Shelter In Faith

Finding the Grace that Holds in the Eye of the Storm

Cynthia Oliver

Whispers & Warfare

Copyright © 2025 by Cynthia Oliver

All rights reserved.

No portion of this book may be reproduced in any form without written permission from the publisher or author, except as permitted by U.S. copyright law.

Contents

Playlist- A Soundrack for the Storms	VII
Introduction For the days you don't feel safe, strong, or seen	XI
A Prayer for the Reader	XV
1. Safe Is Not Comfortable (Unfortunately) Day 1	1
2. Safe in the Storm (Even When It Doesn't Stop) Day 2	9
3. Safe in His Name (Not Your Google Search History) Day 3	18
4. Safe Doesn't Mean Unshaken Day 4	25
5. Safe from Shame Day 5	34

6.	Safe When You're Seen Day 6	44
7.	Safe Doesn't Mean Silent Day 7	55
8.	Safe in the Waiting Day 8	65
9.	Safe When You're Called Out Day 9	74
10.	Safe in Surrender Day 10	83
11.	Safe from the Snare Day 11	92
12.	Safe to Be Weak Day 12	100
13.	Safe in the Fire Day 13	109
14.	Safe When You're the Black Sheep Day 14	120
15.	Safe When God Feels Silent Day 15	130

16.	Safe When You're Crushed Day 16	139
17.	Safe In The Struggle to Forgive Day 17	148
18.	Safe in the Sorrow Day 18	159
19.	Safe When You Start to Rebuild Day 19	170
20.	Safe When You're the Strong One Day 20	180
21.	Safe In Success Day 21	191
22.	Safe When You Lose It All Day 22	201
23.	Safe in The Secret Struggles Day 23	210
24.	Safe When You're Angry with God Day 24	221
25.	Safe When You Doubt Your Faith Day 26	232

26.	Safe When You're Tempted to Numb Out Day 25	242
27.	Safe When You're Spiritually Exhausted Day 27	252
28.	Safe in the Stretch (From Faith to Faith) Day 28	263
29.	Safe in the Victory You Didn't Expect Day 29	274
30.	Safe in Salvation Day 30	284
31.	Final Word: You are Forever Safe Finished	296

Forever Grateful I thank God	301
About the author	303

Playlist- A Soundrack for the Storms

1. The Shelter

- "Unto You" – Eastgate Worship
- "Run to the Father" – Cody Carnes
- "Yhwh" – Cross Timbers Worship
- "Quiet" – Elevation Rhythm
- "Take Courage" – Bethel Music & Kristene DiMarco

2. Safe in the Sorrow

- "In the Room" – Maverick City x UPPERROOM
- "When the Tears Fall" – Tim Hughes
- "Better Word" – Leeland
- "Gratitude" – Brandon Lake
- "I'll Give Thanks" – Housefires

3. The Waiting Room

- "Wait on You" – Elevation Worship & Maverick City Music

- "Not in a Hurry" – Will Reagan & United Pursuit

- "Jesus Be The Name" – Elevation Worship, Tiffany Hudson

- "Seasons" – Hillsong Worship

- "Promises" – Maverick City Music

4. The Battle Belongs

- "Battle Belongs" – Phil Wickham

- "No Longer Slaves" – Bethel Music

- "Raise a Hallelujah" – Jonathan & Melissa Helser

- "Always on Time" – Bella Cordero with Elevation Worship

- "Reckless Love" – Corey Asbury

5. The Rescue

- "At the Altar" – Elevation Rythm ft. Tiffany Hudson

- "Too Good to Not Believe" – Brandon Lake
- "Proof – Live" –Seth Addison, Sophiia Homrighausen
- "Rest on Us" – Maverick City Music
- "Tend" – Bethel Music

6. The Revival

- "Have My Heart" – Maverick City Music
- "Fresh Wind" – Hillsong Worship
- "You Hold It All Together" – Maverick City Music & Upperroom
- "Breakthrough" – Red Rocks Worship
- "Sweep Me Away" – Kari Jobe

7. The Benediction

- "The Blessing" – Elevation Worship, Kari Jobe, Cody Carnes
- "Break Every Chain" – Jesus Culture
- "Goodness of God" – Bethel Music

- "Worthy of It All" – David Brymer
- "All of My Heart" – Chris Martin, Demi Martin

INTRODUCTION

There's something sacred about finally admitting you don't feel safe.

Not physically, necessarily, though maybe that too. But emotionally. Spiritually. Mentally. In your body. In your relationships. In your thoughts.

In the quiet parts of your life where the panic whispers, *"It's all on you. Don't fall apart now. No one is coming."*

We're taught to be strong. To hold it together. To keep the mask on and the volume down. To spiritualize our survival and call it "trust."

But what if we've been equating strength with silence and calling it faith?

What if the most powerful thing you can do today is stop performing and start *sheltering*? That's where this devotional begins:

Not at the surface. But in the ache. In the moment where the waves rise and the bottom falls out, and your soul is whispering, *"Where is safety when life keeps breaking?"*

Shelter Isn't an Escape, It's a Person

We have all read Psalm 91. This isn't a metaphor for people with easy lives.

This is a promise for the wrecked, the raw, the ones who've lost track of what peace even feels like.

To *shelter in place* with God means you stop running. You stop trying to earn rest. You stop looking for a way out and instead run to the only One who *was never shaken to begin with.*

The safest place you can be isn't the life you planned, the prayer you're still waiting on, or the outcome you're trying to control.

It's in Him. In His Word. In His presence. In His shadow, where you get to exhale and say, *"I don't have to hold this anymore. You're holding me."*

What You're Carrying Isn't Yours to Carry Alone

Maybe you're carrying something that feels too heavy to name.

Or maybe you've stopped talking about it because people expect you to be "over it" by now.

You love Jesus, but you're also exhausted.

You believe in hope, but your anxiety has a megaphone.

You're showing up for your life, but inside you're asking: "Is there a place where I'm actually safe to unravel?"

Yes. That place is here. And His name is **Jesus**. You can trust your everything to Him.

This devotional isn't about becoming stronger.

It's about realizing you already have a **refuge**.

You don't have to build one. You just have to walk into it.

This isn't a workbook to fix you. It's not a Bible study to test you. It's not spiritual Pinterest. It's a place for your real self to come undone, in the safest hands that ever existed. The God who sees you. Who rescues you.

Who knows how tired you are, how much you've tried, and how deeply you're longing to feel *safe* again.

Each day will meet you in that longing.

It will explore what safety looks like in the middle of storms, shadows, surrender, silence, waiting, weakness, and wild grace.

And it will keep reminding you:

- You are safe to grieve.

- Safe to hope again.

- Safe to heal slowly.

- Safe to not have it all together.

- Safe to speak, to feel, to rest.

- **Safe to come home to God—again and again and again.**

So here's your invitation.

Not to be better. Not to do more. Just to **shelter in place.**

You are safe here. Even in the mess. Even in the middle. Even in the moments where safety feels impossible, **you're already held.**

The shelter isn't just a place.

It's a Person. And He never leaves.

A Prayer for the Reader

Jesus,

You see them.

Every single one.

The one scrolling late at night with tired eyes and a broken heart.

The one who grew up in church but never really knew You. The one who knows every worship song but still feels far away. The one who's been searching for safety in people, plans, pills, performance, only to come up empty. The one who was handed trauma and told to call it faith. The one who was handed religion but never relationship.

You see the hungry ones, the hurting ones. The ones who still aren't sure if You're real, or if You're really good.

And yet you brought them here.

To these pages.

To this devotional.

To this holy invitation.

So Jesus, we ask boldly:

Let this not be just another devotional. Let this be a rescue. Let these pages light up with the truth of who You are.

You are:

The Only Way to the Father

The Only Name that saves.

The Only Shelter that will never collapse.

Holy Spirit, fall fresh on every person who touches this book. Whether they open it in faith or curiosity, interrupt their silence with Your presence. Ignite a hunger that nothing else can satisfy.

Break every chain that's tried to choke out their purpose. Overthrow every lie that says they've gone too far or waited too long.

Breathe fire into dry bones.

Breathe peace into panic.

Breathe new life into every heart that's dared to hope again.

We ask for salvation. Real. undeniable, tear-stained salvation.

We ask for hearts to say even through trembling lips:

Jesus, I believe You died for me, I believe You rose again. You are the Son of God. You are my Savior. I surrender. Come live in me. Be my shelter. Be my safe place. Be my Lord.

May that prayer rise up in bedrooms and kitchens, break rooms and coffee shops, and churches in the hidden places no one sees.

God we pray Your Word would go to war on their behalf. Let Psalm 91 wrap around them like armor. Let the shadow of the Almighty silence the enemy's lies. Let Your voice be louder than shame. Let Your presence be felt, like heat, like weight, like shelter in a storm.

Keep them safe. Not just in body, but in soul. Keep them safe from deception, from discouragement, from distraction. and when the storms come, and they will, remind them that being safe doesn't mean untouched. It means undone in Your love and held through the waves.

God, for the one holding this devotional with hands that shake, the one thinking " this can't be for me" , the one who's halfway out the door of their faith. Grab their heart. Surround them. Saturate them. Interrupt their exit plan with holy love. Father we know you leave the 99 for the one and this? This might be their one moment. Let them know they are seen, they are wanted, and they are safe, because You are the One holding them now.

Jesus, seal this devotional with your blood. Mark every page. Anoint every prayer. Cover every reader. Let this be more than words. Let it be a meeting place. Where chains fall, hearts soften, and new life begins.

In the mighty, matchless, fire-filled, healing name. of Jesus

Amen

Day 1

SAFE IS NOT COMFORTABLE (UNFORTUNATELY)

"Whoever dwells in the shelter of the Most High will rest in the shadow of the Almighty." Psalm 91.1

LET'S BE REAL: WHEN you hear the word "safe", you probably imagine being curled up on the couch with a fuzzy blanket, a snack that definitely wasn't part of your diet plan, and a "Do Not Disturb" sign hanging from your forehead. That kind of safety is warm, cozy, and if we are honest, it usually involves carbs.

But the Bible has a frustrating way of redefining words we thought we understood.

Psalm 91:1 talks about dwelling in the shelter of the Most High and finding rest in His shadow. that sounds peaceful, right? Until you realize that the shelter implies there's something out there worth hiding from. Shadows mean there's heat somewhere trying to scorch you. So while it sounds poetic, what this verse is actually saying is " Hey, stuff is gonna get crazy, but you can rest because of who's with you."

Biblical safety is not the absence of trouble; it's the presence of God in the middle of it.

And that? Thats not always comfortable.

Sometimes being safe in God means walking into situations you would've preferred to avoid, messy family drama, breakups that crack your heart in half, a diagnosis that reroutes your entire year, or the death of a dream you were sure God gave you. You might still feel unsafe in every human sense of the word. But here's the wild truth: You are still Safe.

Because "safe" in God's eyes means your soul is covered. Your eternity is secure. Your story is being written by hands that cannot fail, even when your current chapter feels like its written in chaos font.

Real Talk: When Comfort Becomes an Idol

We don't like discomfort. We will do just about anything to avoid it.

Distract ourselves with scrolling.

Numb ourselves with busyness or binge-watching.

Pretend everything is find while quietly unraveling inside.

But here's the thing; comfort is a terrible god. It promises peace but delivers passivity. It keeps you stuck where it's familiar instead of moving where God is calling your. And ironically, the more we chase comfort, the less safe we actually feel.

Biblical safety might lead you into the lion's den (ask Daniel) or onto a battlefield with no armor (...David). But it always comes with this quiet promise.

"I am with you. I've got you. You are NOT alone."

What Are You Calling Safe?

Let's ask a hard question: What are you calling safe that's actually just familiar?

Some of us stay in unhealthy situations, patterns, or mental spaces because at least we know that to expect there. We mistake predictability for protection. We keep showing up for jobs, relationships, or belief systems that don't honor our calling simply because we've labeled them "safe."

God doesn't promise safe the way the world defines it. He offers something better: Himself. And when you're dwelling in His shelter, even when life feels like it's falling apart; He holds you together.

Let this sink in:

You are not safe because life is predictable.

You are not safe because your health is perfect.

You are not safe because your relationships are peaceful or your finances are secure.

You are safe because the God of heaven is your dwelling place. Because the shadow of the Almighty covers you ike an invisible forcefield that shields your soul even when your circumstances try to shake it.

So, No, safe is not always comfortable. but it is deeply secure. and the longer you walk with God, the more you'll realize: It's better to be uncomfortable n His will, than to feel cozy outside of it.

God,
I've bee chasing the kind of safe that doesn't last, the kind that numbs me, distracts me, and keeps me small. But I want Your version of safety. The kind that walks me through fire but never lets me burn. the kind that anchors me when the wind picks up. The kind that trades my fear for faith.

I confess, I've made comfort my priority and called it wisdom. I've settles for survival instead of leaning into Your presence. But today, I want to dwell in You, not just visit on Sundays or when I'm desperate. Show me how to rest in Your shadow. Teach me that being close to You is the safest place I could ever be, even if everything else is shaking.

You are my refuge. You are my strong tower. And I choose to run to You, not because I have it all together, but because I don't. Thank you for being the kind of God who doesn't promise an easy life, but promises to never leave me in it.

In Jesus' name
Amen.

Journal Prompts

What does "safe" look like to you right now?

Is there an area of your life where you've been chasing comfort instead of God?

Ask God to show you where He wants you to dwell, even if it stretches you.

Safe in the Storm (Even When It Doesn't Stop)

"He got up rebuked the wind and said to the waves, 'Peace! Be still' Then the wind dies down and it was completely calm." Mark 4:39

Jesus said " Let's go to the other side," and the disciples got in the boat with Him.

Seems simple, right? Jesus said go, they went.

But here's what Jesus didn't mention in that little invitation to adventure. There would be a storm waiting halfway across. And not just some "cute peaceful, lets watch a movie" kind of storm.

No.

It was a violent, wave swallowing, heart in your throat storm. And where was Jesus?

Sleeping.

This is where i think we get it confused, a storm doesn't always mean you did something wrong.

One of the first lies we believe when the wind starts howling in our lives is this:

"I must have done something wrong."

But the disciples weren't in the storm because they disobeyed. They were in the storm because they obeyed.

They followed Jesus straight into a storm, and he knew it. He invited them anyway.

Thats a hard truth to swallow. We like to believe that obedience to God equals a smooth ride. Like, "Hey God, I said yes to You. Can you maybe not let my whole life fall apart now?"

But real talk?

Following Jesus doesn't mean your bot won't get rocked. It means your boat won't sink, because He's in it.

Let that sink in for just a moment.

It's one thing to be in a storm. It's another to feel like God's asleep while you are drowning. The disciples are panicking, and Jesus is out cold on a cushion. The contrast is wild.

They wake Him up with a question that most of us have whispered in the dark: "Don't you care if we drown?"

Let's just take a pause on that.

That question wasn't just about water. It was about trust. It was a cry of "How can you be so calm when I am falling apart?"

It was an accusation wrapped in fear.

We've all been there. Maybe you are there now.

Maybe your storm isn't thunder and waves, it's grief. Its anxiety. It's betrayal. It's another bill you can't pay. It's parenting exhaustion, health fear, spiritual numbness, relational heartbreak.

And you are looking at Jesus like, "You see this, right? You're going to do something.. right?"

That storm reveals your foundation, and the crazy part?

The disciples had already seen Jesus perform miracles. They'd seen Him cast out demons, heal the sick, teach with power. But in the storm, they panicked like strangers.

Why?

Because storms don't just shake your circumstances. They shake your faith foundation.

Storms reveal what you really believe about God.

Is He good only when life is good?

Is He powerful only when your prayers get answered the way you want?

Is He faithful only when things go your way?

Or is He still God, still trustworthy, when it's 3 am and you're exhausted, crying, and scared out of your mind?

I have news.. brace yourselves.

He is still in the boat.

Jesus wakes up and doesn't rebuke the disciples first, he rebukes the storm.

Peace. Be still.

The wind listens. The waves go still. And then, He turns to the disciples.

"Why are you so afraid? Do you have such little faith?"

The question isn't cruel, its surgical. Jesus is asking: "After all you have seen Me do, do you still think I'll let you drown?"

Here's the truth: the storm might not leave right away.. But He never will.

And your safety doesn't come from the calm. It comes from the company.

He was there before the waves.

He was there during the storm.

And He will be there after it all clears.

What is the storm is the tool?

What if it is revealing the parts of you that still don't trust God?

What if it's pulling back the curtain on the false security you've built around your job, your health, your relationships, or your bank account?

What if the storm is shaking off everything that was never supposed to carry you in the first place?

And what if, right there, windblown, scared, and soaked, you finally realize: He's enough.

Jesus,

I confess, I don't like the storm, I don't like the waiting, the unknown, the fear. when things feel out of control I assume You've forgotten me. Or worse, that You don't care. But deep down, I know that is not true.

You are not distant. You are not asleep in the way I fear. You are steady, even when the waves roar.

Help me stop measuring Your love by the size of my problems. Help me stop panicking when You're not moving the way I want You to. Teach me to trust that Your presence is my peace; even if the waves don't go away right now.

And when the storm reveals my shaky faith, don't let my shame take over. Use it to build me. Use it to draw me closer. You are my anchor, my shelter, my calm.

And even here, I am safe.

In Jesus name,

Amen

Journal Prompts

What storms are you currently facing?

How have you been interpreting God's silence? Have you mistaken it for absence or abandonment?

What parts of your faith are being tested or revealed?

SAFE IN HIS NAME (NOT YOUR GOOGLE SEARCH HISTORY)

"The name of the Lord is a strong tower, the righteous run to it and are safe." Proverbs 18:10

YOU KNOW WHATS WILD?

We will run to just about anything or anyone before we run to God.

We run to our phones. To distraction. To a Google rabbit hole that started with "mild chest pain" and ends with writing your own eulogy.

We run to people who make us feel seen even if they don't love us well. We run to food, busyness, control, sarcasm (stepping on my own toes here... and it hurts), social media, or silence.

And then we wonder why we still feel so unsafe. Why peace never settles, why anxiety simmers just beneath the surface, why we keep spiraling.

But Proverbs 18:10 paints a different picture. It says "the name of the Lord is a strong tower." Not just a wall. Not a hedge. Not a little spiritual panic room.

A tower.

Tall. Sturdy. Unshakable.

The kind of place you run to when the war breaks out. When arrows fly. When your heart is in pieces and the enemy is closing in.

And here's the catch: the verse doesn't say the righteous are safe. It says they run to God's name and there they are safe.

Running is a choice.

Running requires movement, intention. Direction.

You don't "accidentally" run to the Lord. You have to choose to.

That means at the moment fear shows up or shame slithers in, or your past comes knocking, you get to choose where your feet go.

You can run bak to numbing.

You can run toward self-sufficiency.

Or you can run to the shelter of His name.

And what does His name even mean?

His Name holds His Nature.

In biblical times, names weren't just labels. They were identities. they revealed character purpose and power.

So when you run to the name of the Lord, you're not just crying out to a vague deity in the sky.

You are running to:

Jehovah Jireh: the God who provides even when your paycheck doesn't stretch and your soul feels starved.

Jehovah Rapha: The God who heals even when the diagnosis is bad and the wound is invisible.

El Roi: the God who sees you, when you feel forgotten and overlooked by the world.

Jehovah Nissi: the God who fights for you, when you're tired of battling on your own.

The safest place you can be is not a season of ease. It's in the character of God. And the more you know His name, the more you'll trust His nature.

Lets sit in this for a minute.

Maybe you have already run to the other places.

Maybe you gave yourself to someone who didn't love you like they promised to.

Maybe you thought success would silence the self doubt.

Maybe you have tried to control everything around you to feel secure, and now you're exhausted and more anxious than ever.

Here's the truth: None of it can hold you.

It might feel like safety in the moment. It might even look holy, disguised as productivity, perfectionism, and "being strong". But at the end of the day, only one tower stands when everything else fails.

And that tower has a name.

Jesus.

Don't get me wrong, this isn't a call to be "more religious." This is a call to run to the God who already sees your mess and still wants you close.

When you cry out His name, it's not a magic word. It's a declaration of surrender. A reminder that He is who He says He is; even when life feels the opposite.

And here's the beautiful mystery: when you run to His name, you don't find condemnation waiting. You find refuge. You find a God who stands taller than your fear, bigger than your shame, and stronger than your grief.

You find safety. Not because the battle isn't real. But because He is.

God,

I've run to so many things that felt safe in the moment, but they didn't last. They didn't heal me. They didn't protect me. They numbed me. Distracted me. Lied to me. And I am tired of trusting things that keep letting me down.

But You, Lord, are my strong tower. You are consistent when my emotions are not. You are faithful when people fail. You are near when fear screams loud.

I want to run to Your name, not just as a last resort but as my first response. Teach me who You are. Show me that Your name isn't just powerful, its personal.

Let me find safety, peace, identity, and truth not in my circumstances, but in You.

You are El Roi. Jehovah Jireh. Jehovah Rapha, And you are Jesus, Savior, Friend, Anchor of my soul.

Thank You for being the safest place I could ever run.

In Your name,
Amen.

Journal Prompts

(it's only day 3. I hope someone out there feels as sore as I feel right now)

What have you been running to lately that's pretending to offer safety but leaves you more anxious or empty?

What part of God's character (His name) do you need to cling to today?

SAFE DOESN'T MEAN UNSHAKEN

"He alone is my rock and my salvation, My stronghold; I will not be greatly shaken."
Psalm 62:2

LET'S CLEAR SOMETHING UP right away: Being a strong Christian does not mean you don't shake. It just means you know where to steady yourself.

Sometimes we confuse spiritual maturity with emotional numbness. We think that if we really trusted God, we wouldn't cry.

We wouldn't have panic attacks.

We wouldn't stay awake at night with our thoughts racing like a hamster, on a wheel fueled by espresso and trauma.

But here's the truth: You can be safe in God and still feel shaken by life.

David, the man after God's own heart, the warrior king, the giant slayer.. said it best. "I will not be greatly shaken."

Not " I will never be shaken."

Not "I feel nothing, I am a holy robot."

But : "Even when I'm rattled, I rooted."

hmmm that took me somewhere..

BTW..Can we stop measuring our faith by our emotions?

You may feel afraid right now.

You may be crying more than praying.

You may be doubting, hurting, overthinking, over functioning, and under sleeping.

And yet, if you're still holding on, still whispering prayers through the tears, still choosing to show up to life even when you'd rather hide...

That's not weak faith.

That's warrior faith.

You're not faithless because you're trembling.

You're human.

You're in a broken world.

And even Jesus shook with sorrow in Gethsemane before He went to the cross.

If He wasn't above the trembling, neither are you. And that doesn't disqualify you from the presence of God. It draws you deeper into it.

Psalm 62:2 says, "He alone is my rock and my salvation, my stronghold."

Let's talk about that word: stronghold.

A stronghold isn't a cozy blanket fort.

Its not a bubbe wrap suite that keeps life from touching you. Its a fortified place. A high impenetrable tower where you're kept secure, even when the battle still rages outside the walls.

God never promised that things woudn't come for you. But he promised they couldn't undo you.

That's what being safe in Him means.

You might shake, but you won't shatter.

I will say, sometimes life hits harder than you expect, and we feel more shaken because we didn't see it coming.

The job loss.

The breakup

The diagnosis.

The betrayal.

The call in the middle of the night.

We weren't prepared. We weren't braced for impact. And suddenly, our sense of "safe" is knocked out from under us.

But this is why we need God to be our rock.

Not our routine.

Not our relationships

Not our income.

Not our ability to keep everything running smoothly.

Because when life punches yu in the throat and the ground beneath you gives way, you need a foundation that doesn't move.

That's what David had. That's what you can have, too.

So shake if you have to, you are allowed.

Jesus isn't disappointed in your trembling. He's not standing up at the top of the stronghold shouting, "Stop crying and climb up already!"

No, He's the God who steps down into your storm. Who walks into the mess with you. Who lets you collapse into Him, messy and trembling.

You don't have to hold it together to be held by God.

He is not fragile. He does not flinch.

Your grief won't scare Him. Your honesty won't offend Him. Your broken prayers won't diquaify you.

In fact, they may be the very thing that ushers you into the safest place of all: His presence.

One more thing.

You may shake. But if your anchor is in God, you will not fall apart beyond repair.

Because your hope is not in things that change. Your hope is in a God who never does.

God,

I'm tired of pretending to be okay when I'm shaking inside. You know the weight I'm carrying . You know the pressure, the fear, the ache. And I don't want to fake my way through this storm, I want to faith my way through it, with You.

You said You're my stronghold. So I'm not going to try to build my own. I'm not going to keep laning on people, plans, or performances that can't hold me.

I run to You. Not because I'm brave but because i'm broken. Not because I'm strong, but because I know You are.

Thank you for being the kind of God who lets me tremble and still calls me safe. Root me in Your love, anchor me in Your truth. and teach me to trust You more than my own feelings.

Even if i shake, I will not fall. You are my rock, You are my stronghold. You are my safe place.

In Jesus' name,

Amen

Journal Prompts

Where do I feel shaken right now?

What am I standing on that might not be solid?

Ask God to show you what stronghold He wants to be for you, right here, in this moment.

Day 5

SAFE FROM SHAME

"For the Scripture says, 'Whoever believes in Him will not be put to shame.'" Romans 10:11

SHAME HAS A VOICE.

It doesn't yell.

It whispers.

It slinks into yur thoughts after a bad decision, a failure, a breakdown.

It shows up after you raise your voice at your kids, after you ghost someone yu care about, after you spiral again even though you swore you wouldn't.

Shame doesn't say, "You made a mistake."

Shame says, "You are the mistake."

And that my friend is exhausting.

You try to drown it out by being productive. Or funny. Or perfect. Or invisible. But no matter how fast you run or how well you perform, it clings like smoke, reminding you of who you used to be, what you wish you could change, or what you're scared people might find out.

But Romans 10:11 hits different.

"Whoever believes in Him will not be put to shame."

Wait... not put to shame?

Even with your past?

Even with the stuff no one knows about?

Even with the parts of you that still feel too messy, too dark, or too broken?

YES.

Because the Gospel is not a behavior modification program. It's not a religious self-help plan. It's a rescue mission. And Jesus didn't die for the polished version of you. He came for the version of you that sits in silence wondering, "Am I still lovable?"

Shame vs. Conviction

Let's not get it twisted, God will convict you.

Conviction is from the Holy Spirit. It says, "That wasnt who you are. Let's grow. Let's turn. Lets rise."

Shame is from the enemy.

It says, " this is who you are. Stay down. Don't even try."

Conviction leads to restoration. Shame leads to isolation.

God never uses shame to heal you. In fact, Jesus bore our shame on the cross. Tha'ts part of what He came to set you free from.

So here's the question of the hour.. Are you building walls or altars?

Shame makes you hide, yes, but it is also a builder, and it builds fast.

Every time someone dismissed your pain...

Everytime your vulnerability was used against you.

Every time someone quoted Scripture like a slap instead of a salve.. You helped shame stack another brick.

A joke to deflect. A silence to avoid. A smile that said, "I'm fine," while your heart screamed, "Please see me." Brick by brick, moment by moment, you've built a wall. Maybe around your trauma, your testimony, or your tenderness. That wall didn't come from pride. It came from protection. because somewhere along the way yu learned its safer to be hidden than to be honest.

Funny thing about those walls, they don't just keep the pain out. the keep God out too. Not because He is unwilling to come close, but because you are too afraid to let Him see the version of you you're still ashamed of. Shame tells you God doesn't want to hear from you until you've "fixed it." It makes church feel like a place for "good people," and worship feel like something for the healed, no the hurting.

And so, we build walls instead of altars. We withdraw when we should be running to God. We stuff it down, smile through it, and tell ourselves, " Next week I'll be better. Then I'll pray."

But God's presence isnt a reward for your perfection. It's the place where shame goes to die. He is standing on the other side of that wall .. Not with condemnation. Not with a wrecking ball. But with mercy in His hands, saying " Let's tear this down together, and build something holy instead."

Shame builds walls. But grace? Grace builds altars.

Altars say: "This is where I met God in my mess." " This is where i laid down the thing I couldn't carry anymore." " This is where He saw all of me, and didn't walk away."

Altars are messy, sacred places.

They're not about who you pretend to be. They're where heaven meets humanity; honestly, imperfectly and powerfully.

Walls or Altars.. one keeps you stuck, the other sets you free.

God's love doesn't flinch. He is not embarrassed by you.

He is not keeping score with a clipboard.

He is not disgusted by your struggle.

He doesn't see you as a project to fix.

He sees you as a child to love.

When Adam and Even sinned, the fist thing they did was cover themselves and hide. But the first thing God did? He came looking for them.

Not to punish.

But to cover.

To call them out of shame and back into relationship. Thats the heartbeat of the Father.

Maybe shame told you:

You're the failure.

You're the addict.

You're the divorce.

You're the mistake.

You're the one whos always too much or never enough.

But God calls you:

Redeemed.

Chosen.

Forgiven.

Called.

Sealed with the Holy Spirit.

A new creation.

And you get to decide wich voice you believe.

Pay attention.... this is where shame ends.

You are safe from shame not because yu never mess us, but because your identity is no longer rooted in performance; it's rooted in Christ.

You are not just tolerated.

You are welcomed.

You are wanted.

You are woven into the story of grace.

You're not holding on to Jesus while hoping shame doesn't catch up. You're held by Him, hidden in Him, safe in Him.

So let this be the day you stop hiding.

Stop apologizing for your existence.

Stop editing your story to look more "acceptable."

Bring the whole mess to Jesus.

Let Him meet you there.

You are not the exception to grace.

You are the reason for it.

God,

Shame has worn me out. It plays on repeat, reminding me of the worst things i have done or believed. It tells me I'm disqualified, dirty, too far gone, or never enough.

But You say I'm safe in You. That I'll never be put to shame when i put my trust in You.

Help me believe that.

Help me silence the voice of the accuser and tune into the voice of the Father. Where shame says "hide," You say "come." Where same says "prove yourself," You say "rest in Me."

Jesus I thank you for covering my shame on the cross. Not just my sin, but the guilt and the voice that tries to haunt me. I don't want to run from You anymore, I want to run to You.

You are the safe place where shame can't live. Remind my heart, again and again, that I am deeply loved, fully known, and never rejected in You.

In Jesus Name

Amen

Journal Prompts

Where has shame been speaking in my life?

What lies am I believing about my worth, identity, or past?

Ask God to show you how He sees you, then write it down as a reminder.

SAFE WHEN YOU'RE SEEN

"Then she called the name of the Lord who spoke to her. 'You are a God who sees me', for she said, 'Have I even seen Him here and lived after He saw me?" Genesis 16:13

BEING SEEN SOUNDS BEAUTIFUL, until you actually are.

There's a version of "seen" that we all crave. The highlight reel kind. The applause, the affirmation, the "Look at how strong she is" kind. The version of your that's admired... but not really known.

Because real seeing?

That's terrifying.

Being truly seen means your guard is down.

Your tone isn't perfect.

Your trauma shows.

Your hands shake.

Your makeup smudges from the tears you swore you weren't going to cry.

Being truly seen means someone might witness the moments you have worked so hard to bury. And deep down, you wonder:

If someone saw all of it, would they still stay?

There are parts of you you've never said out loud.

Not to your family.

Not to your pastor.

Not even to your best friend.

Maybe it's something that was done to you.

Maybe it's something you did and still can't forgive yourself for.

Maybe it's not one big thing, just a long, exhausting list of quiet disappointments that have shaped how you see yourself.

And even now, you keep a part of you back.

Because the lies have lingered too long:

"You're too much."

"You're a burden."

"You're only loved when you are useful."

"If they knew the real you, they'd leave."

So you have learned how to be seen... but not known.

Maybe you haven't thought about it like that before, but you've been running.

Not physically(unless you have) but emotionally. Spiritually. Relationally.

You have been editing yourself to be more palatable. Shrinking in rooms you should take up space in. Apologizing for having... emotions.. of all things. Performing because perfection feels safer than presence.

You love God, but if you're honest, you don't fully trust Him with the real you.

You trust Him with your worship songs, your prayer requests, your quiet time journal. But not the part of you that still cries over things that happened a decade ago. Not the part that sometimes doubts He even sees you at all.

But then...Hagar

Hagar wasn't anyone's first choice.

She wasn't chosen. She was used.

A slave, passed around like a solution to someone else's problem. When things got messy, she wasn't protected, she was pushed out.

Alone.

Pregnant.

Rejected.

Fleeing into a wilderness with no plan and no home.

And that is where God found her.

Not in a church. Not in a temple.

In her flight. In her shame. In her exile.

And He didn't just see her circumstances; He saw her. And He knew her.

By name.

With compassion.

With no condemnation in His voice.

With a future in His hand.

"You are a God who sees me." Genesis 16:13

That's the moment everything changed for her.

Not because her situation was fixed right away. But because someone finally saw her and stayed.

You Are Not Too Much

This is where it gets personal.

God sees you.

Not the you that you curate.

Not the cleaned-up, polished, people-pleasing version.

Not the "strong for everyone else" you.

He sees the one who didn't sleep last night.

The one still haunted by what they don't talk about.

The one who cries behind the steering wheel before pulling herself together to walk into work.

The one who's exhausted from holding everything and everyone together.

He sees the fear.

The rage.

The emptiness you've never fully admitted.

The part of you that secretly wonders, *"Am I too far gone?"*

And guess what??? He doesn't flinch. He doesn't leave. He doesn't look away.

Why?? You are safe...even here.

He Doesn't Want the Mask

God doesn't want the version of you that you think He prefers.

He wants the real one.

The one who feels numb during worship.

The one who avoids prayer because the silence hurts too much.

The one who keeps busy so they don't fall apart.

And when you finally bring yourself to Him, the unedited version, He wraps you up in grace, not shame.

You don't have to prove anything.

You don't have to get it all sorted before you show up.

You just have to stop running.

Because the place you've been hiding?

It's not protecting you anymore.

It's *isolating* you from the One who already sees and still stays.

Being Seen Doesn't Mean Being Shamed

You've spent so long believing that if someone really saw you, they'd leave.

But Jesus already sees, and He's still here.

This is where healing starts.

Not when the pain is gone, but when you stop hiding.

You are not a burden.

You are not "too much."

You are not only valuable when you're helping everyone else.

You are not unsafe to love.

You are not a project.

You are not past the point of being pursued.

You are a daughter or a son.

Fully seen.

Fully known.

And fully loved.

Prayer: For you to come out of hiding
God, I'm scared to be seen.
I've lived a lot of my life managing impressions.
Trying to be lovable. Trying to be safe.
Trying to be enough for everyone else so I didn't have to face the fear that I might not be.
But You see me.
You saw Hagar in her exile. You saw her when no one else wanted her. And You didn't just notice her, you named her. You gave her purpose.
Do that for me.
See the parts I've kept hidden. The memories I don't say out loud. The pain I try to suppress. The questions I'm scared to ask.
And instead of turning away, stay.
Show me that I'm safe to be known.
Safe to be real.
Safe to fall apart in Your arms.
And safe to be rebuilt, not in shame, but in love.
I don't want to hide anymore.
See me, Lord. And heal me here.
In Jesus' name,
Amen.

Journal Prompt:

What parts of me do I keep hidden, even from God?

What would it look like to let Him see *all* of me, without the fear of rejection?

Write as if you're telling Him everything, what hurts, what you wish you could say, what you're scared to feel, and then ask Him to see you, and show you what He sees.

SAFE DOESN'T MEAN SILENT

"I sought the Lord, and He answered me, And rescued me from all my fears." Psalm 34:4

THERE'S A VERSION OF you that learned to stay quiet.

Not because you didn't have something to say; but because somewhere along the way, speaking up felt unsafe.

Maybe your voice was shut down, mocked, ignored, or misunderstood. Maybe when you did open your heart, it got used as ammo. Maybe you were told to "get over it," "pray it away," or "stop being dramatic."

So you stopped talking.

Not just with people—but with God, too.

It wasn't that you stopped believing in Him. You just didn't know if you were allowed to be *that honest*. You didn't know if your voice still mattered when your prayers weren't being answered the way you hoped.

You may have kept worshiping, going to church, posting Scripture. But silence crept into the deepest parts of your soul—the parts you don't show anymore.

About this time is when the enemy steals your voice. Let's be clear: the enemy *loves* your silence.

Because if he can't keep you from believing in God, he'll try to keep you from actually engaging with Him.

He'll convince you that prayer only "counts" if it sounds poetic, polished, or problem-free.

He'll whisper things like:

• *"God already knows, so why bother?"*

• *"You've prayed about this enough."*

• *"If God wanted to fix it, He would have by now."*

• *"Other people have it worse. Be grateful and move on."*

And just like that, your connection with God gets quieter.

Not non existent; just... surface-level.

You say you're fine.

You say the right words.

But you've stopped seeking with your *whole* heart.

Because some part of you doesn't feel safe being that vulnerable with Him anymore.   **But David Did**

Psalm 34:4 says:
"I sought the Lord, and He answered me, and rescued me from all my fears."

David was no stranger to fear.

Or betrayal. Or heartbreak. Or loneliness.

But he didn't let those things shut his mouth.

He *sought* the Lord.

He *spoke* to Him.

He poured out the raw, unfiltered truth of his soul again and again and again.

And what did God do?

He answered.

He rescued.

Not always instantly.

Not always in the way David hoped.

But always with presence.

Always with power.

Always with love.

I have news..you Don't Have to Censor Yourself with God

Let's settle this once and for all: **God is not intimidated by your honesty.**

If you're mad, tell Him.

If you're doubting, say it.

If you're scared, confused, numb, tired, anxious, overwhelmed—say the whole messy thing out loud.

Because healing doesn't start with pretending.

It starts with **truth**. And the safest place to tell the truth is in the presence of the One who *is* Truth.

You were never meant to be a quiet Christian suffering behind a smile.

You were meant to be in **constant communion** with a God who already knows and still says, "Come closer. Let's talk.

What if you believed that the presence of God wasn't just a holy place, but a **safe place**?

What if you stopped waiting until you "felt more spiritual" and just started talking again?

You don't have to explain yourself.

You don't have to rehearse the right words.

You don't need a journal, a worship playlist, or the perfect mood.

You just need your voice.

Even if it trembles.

Even if it cracks.

Even if it's barely more than a whisper.

God wants your voice.

He wants your fear-soaked questions.

He wants your exhausted prayers.

He wants the version of you that stopped speaking because life got too heavy and hope got too quiet.

You're not a burden.

You're a beloved child with a Father who listens; even when all you can do is groan.

If You've Been Silent...

If you've stopped talking to God, really talking, not just the safe phrases, this is your invitation to begin again.

You are safe to speak.

You are safe to feel.

You are safe to cry.

You are safe to ask.

And not only that—**you are heard.**

Prayer:
God, I've been quiet—not because I don't believe in You, but because I wasn't sure I could be this honest. I didn't know if You wanted to hear it all—the questions, the pain, the anger, the disappointment. But You do.

You are not a distant judge. You're a loving Father. You're a safe place for me to collapse and confess. You invite me into the kind of relationship that's built on truth, not performance. So here I am. No filter. No script. I want to talk to You again.

Really talk. Not just throw out religious phrases, but actually open my heart.

Even if it's bruised. Even if it's messy. Rescue me from the fear that says I have to stay quiet. Restore the intimacy I've missed. Remind me that I am safe to speak and that You are still listening.

Thank You for always being a God who leans in.

In Jesus' name,

Amen.

Journal Prompt:

Have I been quiet with God lately?

What am I afraid will happen if I start being honest with Him again?

Write a raw, unfiltered prayer. No editing. No censoring. Just truth.

Day 8

SAFE IN THE WAITING

"Yet those who wait for the Lord Will gain new strength; They will mount up with wings like eagles, They will run and not get tired, They will walk and not become weary." Isaiah 40:31

WAITING CAN FEEL LIKE punishment. Whether you're waiting for healing, direction, restoration, provision, or just *relief*, it can be agonizing. Time slows down. Prayers feel stale.

The silence of heaven grows heavy, and you start wondering if God left your request on "read."

And worse? People around you seem to be *getting* the very things you're asking for.

Their breakthrough came.

Their prayer was answered.

Their dream came to life.

You're left watching from the sidelines, smiling through gritted teeth, whispering, "I'm happy for you" while screaming inside, *But God, what about me?*

Beware of the lies that surface in the waiting.

When God doesn't move how or when we want, it's not just disappointing; it's disorienting. And in that disorientation, lies creep in:

- "If God really loved me, He'd fix this."
- "Maybe I didn't pray hard enough."
- "Maybe I'm being punished."
- "What if nothing's ever going to change?"

You start to feel *unsafe* in the waiting; not because God has changed, but because you're no longer sure what He's doing. Or if He's even still listening.

But Isaiah 40:31 offers something radical. It doesn't say those who wait get forgotten. It says they get **renewed**.

Don't confuse the waiting room for the wilderness.

We treat waiting like dead space.

But in God's kingdom, **waiting is a workshop.**

It's where strength is built.

Where clarity sharpens.

Where pride dies and trust deepens.

The Hebrew word used for "wait" in Isaiah 40:31 isn't passive. It's *qavah*—to expect, to look eagerly, to bind together.

So to wait for the Lord isn't sitting on your hands hoping He remembers you.

It's wrapping yourself around His promises.

It's saying, "Even if I don't see it yet, I'll keep trusting You're still moving."

Because He is.

Remember: You're Not Stuck—You're Held

Maybe you're thinking, *This all sounds great in theory, but what about when the waiting drags on for years? What about unanswered prayers that have aged alongside me?*

That's fair.

And still; this truth remains:

The longer the wait, the more personal the formation.

God is not making you wait as punishment.

He's protecting you from settling too soon.

He's strengthening your roots so that when the breakthrough comes, it doesn't destroy you, it builds you.

And even now, while it feels like nothing is happening, you are not *stuck*.

You are **held**.

Ask Abraham. Ask Joseph. Ask Jesus.

Abraham waited decades for the promise of a son.

Joseph waited in a pit, then a prison, while his dreams sat in limbo.

Jesus waited 30 years before stepping into public ministry; and even then, He waited in the garden for the Father's will to unfold.

If waiting meant abandonment, those stories would look very different.

But they didn't just wait—they waited **with God**.

And that made all the difference.

Because waiting *with* God is not empty.

It's sacred.

It's safe.

What happens when the only answer is "Wait"

Let's be honest: sometimes we just want the pain to end.

We want resolution, not a reminder. We want the "yes" or the "no", not the *not yet*. But what if "wait" doesn't mean "no"?

What if it means, "Not like this. Not yet. Not without more healing. Not without preparing the way." What if the waiting is actually His mercy?

You may never understand all of it.

But you don't have to understand it to be *safe* in it.

Because the promise is not just strength—it's **new** strength.

Strength that lifts, carries, and keeps you standing when your heart feels like collapsing.

Prayer:
God, the waiting has worn me down.
Sometimes I believe You'll come through—but other times, I'm just tired. Tired of hoping. Tired of asking. Tired of watching everyone else's prayers get answered while mine feel suspended in silence.
But I don't want to let this season make me bitter. I want it to make me **bound to You.**
So help me wait well. Not passively. Not fearfully. But with expectancy, even when I'm scared. Even when I don't see movement. Even when I'm tempted to give up.
You said those who wait on You would renew their strength, not lose it. So I'm holding You to that promise.
Remind me that I'm not abandoned. I'm not forgotten. I'm not stuck; I'm being shaped. Make this waiting room a place of worship. Make this hallway holy.
And when I can't run, teach me to walk. When I can't walk, teach me to rest. But never let me stop trusting that You are good, *even here.*
In Jesus' name,
Amen.

Journal Prompt:

Where am I currently waiting for God to move?

What emotions or lies have surfaced during this season?

What might God be building in me that I cannot yet see?

SAFE WHEN YOU'RE CALLED OUT

"He said, 'Come!' And Peter got out of the boat and walked on the water, and came toward Jesus." Matthew 14:29

THERE'S SOMETHING TERRIFYING ABOUT being called out. Not in the "I got roasted in the group chat" way. In the holy way.

In the way where God puts His finger on your heart and says, "Come. Step out of what's familiar. Walk with Me here."

And suddenly all your false security shakes. Your excuses shrivel.

Your control slips. And you're left with this impossible invitation:

Will you trust Me, here, on the waves?

That's what happened to Peter.

He was safe in the boat. Familiar chaos, sure, but at least it was wood and structure and something under his feet.

And then Jesus says *one word* that undoes everything: **"Come."**

Being Called Out Is Exposing

Let's be honest: we hate being called out.

It feels vulnerable. Confrontational. Risky.

Whether it's God convicting your pride, asking you to leave a relationship, nudging you to forgive someone who hasn't apologized, or pressing on that dream you're too scared to chase, it feels like a spotlight on your weakness.

And sometimes, being called out looks like being pulled out.

Out of toxic patterns. Out of shallow faith. Out of comfort zones you've turned into cages.

Peter didn't get called out because he was failing.

He got called out **because he was ready to walk in something deeper.**

And the same might be true for you.

God's Call Isn't to Shame You; It's to Shape You

When God calls you out, He's not scolding. He's inviting. He's saying, "I know this feels impossible, but *I'm out here...come be with Me.*"

But let's not romanticize the moment: Peter walked *on water.*

That's not safe. That's not logical. That's not the route you take when you need predictability and five-year plans.

Yet Jesus didn't hand Peter a life vest.

He handed him **presence.**

Because Jesus knows what we forget: **Your safety isn't found in the boat—it's found in Him.**

When You Sink in the Middle

Peter was doing it. He was walking. He was literally defying physics with his eyes on Jesus.

But the wind picked up. His fear took over. He started sinking.

Cue the inner critic: *See? You shouldn't have tried. You're not strong enough. You'll always fail.*

But Jesus?

He *immediately* reached out His hand.

Not after Peter fixed his posture.

Not after he said the right prayer.

Not after he proved his faith.

> "**Immediately** Jesus reached out His hand and took hold of him..." (v. 31, NASB)

That's the kind of Savior we have.

One who lets us walk on water; but doesn't let us drown in doubt.

One who calls us out; but catches us when we fall.

Sometimes you have to ask "What's Your Boat?"

Let's go deeper. What's your boat?

The thing you've built to feel in control.

The habit.

The relationship.

The version of "God" that doesn't stretch you too much.

The numbness you use to avoid the ache.

Jesus is calling you out of that.

Not because He wants to terrify you, but because He knows there's **more**.

There's life beyond survival.

There's faith beyond formulas.

There's intimacy on the water that the boat will never offer. And yes, it'll cost you certainty.

But what you'll gain?

Him.

The kind of SAFE that knows He Won't Let You Drown

You might be scared right now.

Scared to step out.

Scared to let go.

Scared to obey.

Scared to trust.

And that's okay.

You're not walking toward a taskmaster.

You're walking toward the one who *knows you're scared* and still calls you *worthy*.

You are safe—even when you feel like you're falling—because **He's already reaching.** The voice that calls you out is the same as the hand that will hold you up. That's the kind of God who calls.

That's the kind of Savior who saves.

Prayer:

Jesus, I hear You calling me, but I'm scared. Stepping out feels like losing everything I've clung to for safety. My plans. My control. My idea of what You *should* do.
But You're not calling me to drown. You're calling me to walk. To trust. To come closer. I admit, I've been clinging to comfort. To old patterns. To old identities.
To the false security of what's "safe." But I want what You have for me, even if it's terrifying.
So give me courage to answer. Give me faith to walk. And when I sink, and I know I will, reach for me like You always do. Don't let me drown in fear or shame. Lift me. Shape me. Stay with me.
You are my safety, not the boat.
You are my anchor, even when I'm walking on waves.
Call me out again. I'm listening.
In Your name,
Amen.

Journal Prompt:

What is God currently calling me out of?

What am I afraid of losing if I step out of the "boat"?

Where do I need to trust that Jesus will meet me, even if I start to sink?

SAFE IN SURRENDER

"Saying, 'Father, if You are willing, remove this cup from Me; yet not My will, but Yours be done.'" Luke 22:42

SURRENDER IS NOT EASY.

It's not romantic. It's not always peaceful.

It's not the neatly packaged spiritual act we sometimes make it out to be.

Surrender is ugly cry territory.

It's knees on the floor.

It's breath caught in your throat.

It's white-knuckling your own plans while whispering, "God, please...don't make me let this go."

And yet... it's also the holiest ground you'll ever stand on.

Because in surrender, **your will dies,** and something eternal is born.

Did you know Gethsemane wasn't quiet?

We picture Jesus in the garden, praying softly under the moonlight. But the scene was *violent.*

He sweat blood.

He fell on His face.

He begged.

> "Father, if You are willing, remove this cup from Me..." *Luke 22:42a, NASB*

That's not resignation.

That's a raw, fully human, deeply honest request.

But then, He says the words that changed eternity:

"Yet not My will, but Yours be done."

And right there, with the cross still ahead and the pain still coming, **Jesus surrendered.**

Not because it was easy.

Not because He didn't feel fear.

But because **He trusted His Father more than His feelings.**

Do you ever wonder why surrender hurts so much?

Because it feels like losing.

Losing control.

Losing outcomes.

Losing the version of life you prayed for and planned around.

Surrender asks you to lay down the relationship you swore would be forever.

The dream you've nurtured for years.

The grudge you swore you'd hold until they "got what they deserved."

The timeline you told God was *perfect*.

And here's what no one tells you:

Surrender often looks like silence first.

God may not give immediate clarity, instant peace, or angel choirs in the background.

Sometimes He just gives you space; and Himself.

So if you think about it.. Surrender is a paradox

You'd think that letting go would make you feel exposed.

But real surrender doesn't leave you empty, it frees you from carrying what was never yours to begin with.

In surrender, **you find safety**. Not because everything suddenly makes sense, but because you've finally placed the weight of your life into the hands of the only One strong enough to hold it.

You stop fighting.

Stop striving.

Stop fixing what only He can redeem.

And somehow, mysteriously...

You begin to breathe again.

You Can Be Honest Here.. in fact thats a MUST

If you're not ready to surrender yet; be honest about it.

Jesus didn't skip straight to "Your will be done."

He wrestled.

He *asked for another way*.

And His Father didn't shame Him for it.

That means you're allowed to say:

- "God, I'm scared."
- "God, this hurts too much."
- "God, I'm not sure I trust You with this yet."

The beauty of surrender is that it doesn't require perfection; just permission.

Not **"I have this all figured out."**

Just **"I'm willing to let You lead."**

Let Go... Even if You Have to Do It With Shaking Hands

You might not feel brave today.

But bravery isn't required for surrender.

Obedience is. God doesn't expect you to let go with joy.

He just asks you to do it with trust.

And He knows how much it costs you.

He knows the internal war.

He sees the wrestle.

He's not rushing your process—He's walking through it with you.

You can surrender while trembling. While weeping.

While whispering through tears, "I don't know how this ends, but I know You're good."

And that's enough.

Prayer:
God, I don't want to pretend. This is hard. Letting go feels like losing. And if I'm honest, part of me still believes that holding on gives me more control than trusting You does.

But I'm tired. Tired of fighting You. Tired of holding what's too heavy. Tired of praying for Your will while living out mine. So here I am. Not polished. Not sure. Not fearless. Just here. Willing to let go; maybe slowly, maybe shakily; but still, letting go.

Jesus, You know what it's like to face something You didn't want, and still say, *"Your will be done."* Teach me how to pray like that. Show me that surrender isn't punishment.

It's protection. It's peace. It's love in its purest form, me trusting that *You* know better, even when I don't understand.

I release it. The thing I can't control. The person I can't fix. The outcome I can't script. Take it, Lord. And take my heart with it. Because I don't just want to give You this situation, I want to give You *me*.

In Jesus' name,
Amen.

Journal Prompt:

What am I afraid to let go of right now?

Where have I been clinging to my will more than God's?

What would it look like to trust Him with the outcome, even if I don't understand the process?

SAFE FROM THE SNARE

"For it is He who rescues you from the net of the trapper and from the deadly plague." Psalm 91:3

TRAPS ARE SNEAKY.

No one walks into one on purpose.

They're designed to be subtle. Hidden. Tempting.

Something laced with just enough truth to get you to step in.

A snare doesn't need to be strong, it just needs to be *well-placed.*

It only has to catch one vulnerable part of you to leave you stuck.

And if we're being honest?

Most of us have walked straight into more than one.

The Kind of Traps That Don't Look Like Traps

The enemy isn't out here with flashing neon signs that say, "Hey! Here's your downfall!"

No, it's more like:

- "They didn't respond to your text, must be something you did." *(Trap: insecurity)*
- "You're the only one who still struggles with this." *(Trap: shame)*
- "You're falling behind. Everyone else is thriving." *(Trap: comparison)*
- "You're too broken. God's probably tired of you." *(Trap: despair)*

These aren't just passing thoughts.

They're **snares**—strategically laid to steal your peace, crush your confidence, and separate you from the truth of God's love.

And when you're tired, stretched thin, or wounded, those lies don't just sound believable—they sound *familiar*.

Lord, Place a net around my mind.

The trapper doesn't go after your physical body first.

He goes after your *mind*.

Because if he can entangle your thoughts,

He can slow your walk.

He can bind your identity.

He can twist your story until you can't tell the difference between conviction and condemnation.

That's why Psalm 91:3 is so powerful:

> *"He rescues you from the net of the trapper."*

Not: *He keeps you from ever stepping into one.*

But: *He pulls you out when you're already caught.*

This is the kind of God we serve.

Plot twist...You Are Not Too Tangled to Be Rescued

Maybe you're there right now.

Stuck in something you didn't see coming.

Bound up in regret, in bitterness, in exhaustion, in fear.

You want to move forward—but your legs are tangled.

You want to believe again—but your thoughts are stuck.

And it feels like the more you pull, the tighter it gets.

The shame. The spiral. The silence.

But this is what the psalmist is trying to show you:

You don't rescue yourself. God does.

He doesn't shame you for getting caught.

He steps into the mess, cuts the net, and carries you out.

Because the net that's strong enough to trap you?

Isn't strong enough to hold Him back.

The Rescue Might Look Like This

Sometimes God's rescue is immediate.

A truth that shatters a lie.

A peace that breaks through the fog.

A door that closes before you step off the cliff.

Other times, it's a *slow unraveling*.

He sits with you in the snare.

He speaks truth gently over the knot of your mind.

He sends people who say, "Hey, you're not crazy—and you're not alone."

Either way, it's still rescue.

And you are still safe.

Because the trap doesn't get the final say—**God does.**

Ask Peter.

Ask David.

Ask the woman caught in adultery.

Peter fell into fear. He denied Jesus three times.

David fell into lust, then deception, then full-blown murder.

The woman in John 8? Publicly dragged, exposed, humiliated.

Each one tangled in their own version of a snare.

And yet, each one **rescued**.

Not because they had it together.

Not because they had a perfect repentance speech.

But because **mercy showed up**.

Rescue doesn't start with you fixing yourself.

It starts with recognizing you *can't*.

And that's the safest, most sacred place to be:

In need.

Seen.

Held.

Prayer:
God,
I didn't mean to get stuck. I didn't see it coming. Or maybe I did—and I walked in anyway. Either way, I'm here now. Tangled. Worn out. A little afraid.
But You are the God who rescues. You don't lecture me while I'm trapped. You step in. You cut through. You call me by name and remind me:
"You are not what caught you. You are Mine."
So I invite You into the mess. Into the lies. Into the pattern I can't seem to break. Into the pain I've stopped talking about.
Come find me here, Lord. Pull me out.
Not just from the trap, but from the belief that I deserved to stay in it. Remind me that freedom isn't earned, it's received. And You've already paid the price.
I don't want to live bound by what You already defeated.
Thank You for being a Rescuer who sees me, comes for me, and never lets the trap win.
In Jesus' name,
Amen.

Journal Prompt:

What lie or trap has been wrapping itself around my mind or identity lately?

How might God be trying to rescue me, from the lie, from the pressure, from the past?

SAFE TO BE WEAK

"And He has said to me, 'My grace is sufficient for you, for power is perfected in weakness.' Most gladly, therefore, I will boast about my weaknesses, so that the power of Christ may dwell in me." 2 Corinthians 12:9

WE LIVE IN A world that celebrates strength.

Get it done. Push through. Hustle harder.

Post the highlight reel and leave the breakdown on "close friends" or buried in a note on your phone.

And so, we learn early:

Weakness is something to overcome, not something to admit.

It's something to hide, apologize for, or decorate with humor and distraction.

But then Paul comes along and says something that completely flips the narrative: "I will *boast* in my weakness."

Wait...what?

When You've Run Out Of Strength

There comes a moment; if you're walking with Jesus long enough, when **your strength runs out.**

The therapy stops helping like it used to.

The job doesn't satisfy.

The smile starts cracking.

The weight you're carrying gets heavier than your arms can handle.

And instead of supernatural adrenaline, instead of instant relief, you're met with this whisper: "My grace is sufficient."

Not, *"I'll fix it instantly."*

Not, *"Here's a step-by-step escape plan."*

But: "My grace is enough for even this."

We have to get this....Weakness Isn't Failure, It's an Invitation

When you hit your breaking point, it's not because God has left.

It's because **He's drawing near.**

There's a kind of intimacy that only comes when you're at the end of yourself.

And it doesn't feel inspirational—it feels scary.

Exposed. Humbling. Too vulnerable to feel spiritual.

But this is where grace does its deepest work.

Not when you impress Him.

But when you collapse *into* Him.

God's power is not attracted to your polished moments.

It *moves* in your weakness.

That anxiety you're ashamed of?

That grief you keep apologizing for?

That burnout you're hiding behind productivity?

That's the place He wants to dwell—not just pass through.

But.. What If You Let Go?

Some of us have been trying so hard to keep it together.

To be strong for everyone.

To be resilient, reliable, "fine."

But what if you laid it all down?

Not forever. Not as a resignation.

But just for now. Just long enough to breathe.

What if you gave yourself permission to be weak, and let **God be strong in you?**

You might be shocked by what you find:

- A deeper kind of rest.

- A love that doesn't flinch.

- A grace that doesn't require performance.

- A Father who is *not disappointed* in your need.

Friend, God Is Not Tired of You

This one's for the person who feels like a burden.

Who keeps breaking down.

Who's sick of being the "needy one."

Who prays, "God, I know You've already helped me with this before, but... I'm still struggling."

Listen closely:

He's not tired of you.

His grace doesn't run on a meter.

His patience doesn't expire.

He's not rolling His eyes every time you come back crying.

He's *waiting*—arms open, still gentle, still safe.

You don't have to pretend anymore.

You don't have to be the strong one.

You get to be **held**.

This is the Most Powerful Thing to Know...

The ones who change the world in the name of Jesus?

They're not the ones who never fall.

They're the ones who know what it means to fall **into grace.**

The ones who say: "I don't have what it takes... but I know the One who does."

That's what God builds His power on.

Not your perfection.

Not your personality.

Your **honesty.**

You are *never* more powerful than when you're fully surrendered.

Prayer:
God,
I'm tired of pretending I'm strong. I've been pushing through. Hiding what hurts. Smiling when I want to fall apart. Trying to be everything for everyone, but forgetting I was never supposed to be.
So here I am.
Exposed. Raw. Done. And in this place, I bring You what I thought disqualified me; my weakness.
Because You said Your grace is enough. You said Your power is perfected right here. So I won't hide it anymore. I won't pretend that I'm okay when I'm not. I won't avoid You because I feel like too much. You are the God who meets me on the bathroom floor. In the middle of the breakdown. In the moment the mask slips. And You don't look away.
Thank You for loving me right here. For holding me. For never requiring me to be strong before coming to You.
Let Your power rise in the places where I've collapsed. Let this weakness become holy ground.
In Jesus' name,
Amen.

Journal Prompt:

Where have I been afraid to admit I'm weak?

What have I been trying to carry that God never asked me to?

Ask Him: "God, what part of me are You inviting to rest in Your strength today?"

Safe in the Fire

"If it be so, our God whom we serve is able to rescue us from the furnace of blazing fire; and He will rescue us from your hand, O king. But even if He does not, let it be known to you, O king, that we are not going to serve your gods or worship the golden statue that you have set up." Daniel 3:17–18

No one volunteers for the fire.

You don't sign up to be burned.

You don't pray for pain.

You don't raise your hand and say, "God, please walk me through devastation to prove You're real."

We pray for miracles.

We hope for breakthrough.

We cry out for peace.

But sometimes... we end up in the furnace anyway.

Sometimes you stand for what's right and get misunderstood.

Sometimes you obey and still get rejected.

Sometimes you pray with all the faith you can muster, and the healing doesn't come. Sometimes the people you loved the most leave, and you're left standing in the ash of what was.

This is the fire.

And yet Scripture dares to tell us something shocking: **You are still safe here.**

Shadrach, Meshach, and Abednego Didn't Know the Ending

We read their story with hindsight.

We know they survive.

We know there's a fourth man in the fire.

We know God shows up.

But they didn't.

All they knew was:

- They refused to bow.

- A furnace was waiting.

- And their God *might not* come through the way they wanted.

And still, they said: *"Even if He does not..."*

Let that sink in.

They walked into the flames with no guarantee, except God Himself.

We Think Safety Means Escape

Let's just tell the truth:

Most of us want a God who *delivers us from* the fire—not one who *meets us in* it. We want rescue that looks like comfort, control, and closure.

But sometimes, safety doesn't look like a way out. Sometimes, safety looks like God stepping into the furnace *with you.*

The fire doesn't prove God abandoned you.

It's often where you see that **He never left.**

Because when you lose everything else, reputation, comfort, the approval of others, you discover the one thing that can never be taken:

His presence.

That Is When the Flames Start to Change You

The fire will change you, but not the way the enemy hopes.

The enemy wants it to destroy your faith.

To make you cynical.

To make you cold.

To make you numb.

But God uses it to **refine you.**

Not because He's cruel. But because **what's real survives the fire**—and what was never meant to stay gets burned off.

Sometimes what the fire consumes is the pride that was killing you slowly.

Sometimes it's the fear that kept you silent.

Sometimes it's the version of God you created in your mind—one who serves your comfort, not your calling.

And somehow, when the smoke clears, you find you're still standing.

Not unburned—but *undestroyed.*

Maybe the Miracle Is You

The miracle isn't always the fire stopping.

The miracle might be:

- That you didn't lose your mind.
- That you can still pray even after that diagnosis.
- That you're still kind even after they left.

- That your heart still beats with hope; even if you whisper it now instead of shout.

God didn't stop the fire for Shadrach, Meshach, and Abednego.

He just made sure it didn't *own* them. In fact, the Bible says when they came out of the furnace, **they didn't even smell like smoke.** (Daniel 3:27)

That's who our God is.

He doesn't just protect your life.

He protects your identity, your soul, your dignity, your calling.

You may have walked through hell, but you don't have to live like you still smell like it.

When God Doesn't Deliver the Way You Hoped

This one's for the one who's praying, "God, where were You?"

You lost someone you loved.

You prayed your heart out.

You believed. You fasted. You worshiped. You spoke Scripture like oxygen.

And it still hurt. It still ended. It still broke.

I can't give you answers for that. No verse will undo grief. No devotional will patch the hole left by loss.

But I can tell you:

You are still safe. Not in the absence of heartbreak. But in the unwavering presence of a God who *still steps into the fire with you.*

And He's not ashamed of your questions.

He's not offended by your pain.

He's not asking you to get over it; He's sitting in the ashes with you.

And the Fire Becomes Holy

There will come a day; maybe not today, when you look back at the fire and say: "That almost killed me. But it also awakened me." Because fire doesn't just burn.

It forges.

It makes something unshakable out of what felt fragile.

The safest people I know have been through the fire, and survived with a tenderness that only God could have preserved.

They're not safe because nothing hurt them. They're safe because they *know* who walks beside them now.

Prayer:
God, I hate the fire.
I hate what it costs.
I hate how it burns.
And if I'm honest, I've begged You to make it stop. To pull me out. To undo the pain. But You haven't left. You've stayed. And sometimes, You've even wept with me.
So if this is where I have to be, Then be here with me, Lord. Remind me that I am still safe...
Even if the fire rages, Even if the pain lingers, Even if the outcome isn't what I prayed for.
You are still good. You are still near. You are still God.
And I trust, not that I'll avoid every fire, but that You will always walk me through it.
Don't let this season waste me. Use it. Refine me. And bring me out not just alive, but marked by You.
In Jesus' name,
Amen.

Journal Prompt:

Where am I walking through fire right now?

What has the fire burned off that I didn't realize was weighing me down?

How has God been present, even when I felt abandoned?

Safe When You're the Black Sheep

"For my father and my mother have forsaken me, but the Lord will take me up."
Psalm 27:10 (NASB)

When You Don't Belong Where You Came From

Some of us grew up in houses that never felt like home.

In families that spoke love but withheld acceptance.

In churches that preached grace but only gave shame.

Or maybe we're walking through seasons right now where the people we *thought* would celebrate us are suspicious of our healing. The people who raised us? Confused by our boundaries.

The friends we once laughed with? Disoriented by our new convictions.

Maybe you've felt it in your bones:

"I'm the black sheep."

The one who didn't play by the rules.

The one who got labeled "too much" or "not enough."

The one who hears *"Who do you think you are?"* echo louder than *"I'm proud of you."*

This devotional is for you.

Because "black sheep" in the eyes of man...Looks a whole lot like *"beloved sheep"* in the hands of the Shepherd.

The Ache of Misunderstood Obedience

Sometimes, following God doesn't come with applause.

It comes with **distance**.

With sideways glances from family members who think you've changed too much.

With silence from friends who don't understand why your boundaries got stronger.

With accusations that you're self-righteous or rebellious, when you're just trying to be obedient.

It hurts. Let's name that.

You're doing the work. You're surrendering. You're healing.

And somehow it makes people uncomfortable.

Why?

Because some people liked you better when you were broken.

Some people only know how to love you *as long as you stay small*.

And now that you're growing, stretching, trusting God with the pain you used to numb it shines a light on their shadows.

You're not self-righteous.

You're just **learning how to breathe outside of dysfunction.**

You're not ungrateful.

You're just **learning how to live loved,** even if it's not from the people you thought would give it first.

When You Don't Fit the Box Anymore

Let's get even more honest.

What happens when the black sheep narrative follows you *into your faith life*?

When your healing journey doesn't look like anyone else's?

When your questions make people uncomfortable?

When you don't worship like the person next to you... or vote like them... or parent like them... or process grief like them?

What happens when even *other Christians* treat you like you're on the outside?

You begin to wonder:

"If I don't belong to them... do I belong to God?"

But here's the truth your soul needs tattooed on it:

You belong to the Shepherd ... not the sheep pen.

Jesus didn't come for the ones who always "fit."

He came for the one who wandered. The one who limped.

The one who couldn't hide their brokenness behind a pretty scroll or rehearsed religion.

> *"What man among you, if he has a hundred sheep and has lost one of them, does not leave the ninety-nine in the open pasture and go after the one which is lost, until he finds it?"* Luke 15:4 (NASB)

You are not forgotten.

You are not disqualified.

You are not disowned.

You are *pursued*.

Safe Doesn't Always Feel Familiar

And maybe that's the whole point.

Maybe the reason it feels so unfamiliar to walk in healing...is because you're stepping out of survival.

Maybe the reason people question your change...is because they got used to you shrinking to keep the peace.

Maybe the reason you feel lonely right now...is because God is **rebuilding your identity** from the inside out, and He needs your full attention.

You're not unsafe, you're *just unfamiliar* with what it feels like to be seen without judgment.

And that's where Jesus comes in.

Not as a judge.

Not as a critic.

Not as a religious performance coach.

But as your Shepherd.

The Shepherd Leaves the 99 for the Black Sheep

Let's be real:

God doesn't need you to clean yourself up, package your pain in a perfect testimony, or "fit in" before He comes close.

He already did.

He comes close **to the black sheep.**

To the one who got pushed out.

To the one who doesn't get invited anymore.

To the one who walks into church and feels invisible.

You are the one He leaves the 99 for.

And when He finds you?

He doesn't scold.

He doesn't shame.

He doesn't say *"Finally."*

He says,

"Come here. You're mine. Let's go home."

Prayer for the Black Sheep
Jesus,
I've spent so much time trying to fit where I was never meant to belong.
I've twisted myself into boxes to keep the peace.
I've swallowed my voice to make others comfortable.
I've worn guilt that wasn't mine to carry.
I've apologized for outgrowing trauma that others are still sleeping in.
But You see me.
You don't need me to be polished.
You just want me to be present.
You've never once required me to be "enough" — just to come when You call.
So here I am.
Bruised.
Tired.
Still sometimes questioning my place.
But I'm choosing to believe I'm safe — even if I don't feel like I belong anywhere else.
I'm safe in You.
In the Shepherd who finds the black sheep and carries her home.
Thank You for not needing me to "look the part" to be loved.
Amen.

Journal Prompts

Have you ever felt like the "black sheep" of your family, church, or friend group? What specific moments or experiences come to mind when you think of feeling misunderstood, excluded, or overlooked?

What has God shown you about your identify that contradicts what others have labeled you as? How can you begin to live from His voice rather than theirs?

What does "safe" feel like to you? Can you think of a moment where you truly felt safe in the presence of God, even when people didn't understand you?

SAFE WHEN GOD FEELS SILENT

"How long, Lord? Will You forget me forever? How long will You hide Your face from me? How long am I to feel anxious in my soul, With grief in my heart all the day?" Psalm 13:1–2a

THERE ARE FEW THINGS more disorienting than God going quiet.

Not because you've stopped believing in Him. Not because you've walked away. But because you've done everything "right" and still, the silence screams louder than any worship lyric.

You've prayed the prayers. You've quoted the verses. You've showed up when you didn't want to.

And yet...Nothing.

No whisper.

No goosebumps.

No confirmation.

No direction.

Just... *quiet*.

And if you're being brutally honest?

It's starting to feel personal.

That is the moment when Heaven feels like a closed door.

You wonder:

"Did I do something wrong?"

"Is He punishing me?"

"Is He tired of me asking the same questions over and over again?"

You scroll past testimonies online, "God told me to quit my job and 4.3 seconds later He dropped a promotion in my lap!" and you're just trying to survive without falling apart.

You sit in church and watch people fall to their knees and hear from God in seconds, while your soul is starving for even the faintest whisper.

You're not angry.

You're just tired.

And if you're honest, a little afraid that maybe this silence means something deeper: *Maybe God really did walk away.*

But...The Silence Isn't a Sign of Abandonment

Let me say this plainly: **God's silence is not His absence.**

It may feel like rejection. But often, silence is the language of **trust**.

Not because He's cruel. But because He's close enough to know you can walk a little further now, *with faith, not feelings.*

The silence isn't a punishment.

It's a sacred pause.

And sometimes, what feels like a delay is actually an invitation.

Not to strive harder.

But to go deeper.

David Felt It Too

David, the man after God's own heart, penned the exact ache you feel: "How long, Lord? Will You forget me forever? How long will You hide Your face from me?" Psalm 13:1

He didn't sugarcoat it.

He didn't wrap it in a bow.

He cried out with frustration and grief, **and still trusted God enough to bring the cry.**

David wasn't disqualified by his questions. He was known by them. And so are you.

God is not offended by your ache.

He's not rolling His eyes at your pain.

He's not keeping score of how many times you've prayed the same thing.

He's holding space for the version of you who feels forgotten, because *He hasn't.*

When Silence Feels Like a Slow Burn

We don't talk about the middle enough.

We love the mountaintop moments. The breakthroughs. The answered prayers.

But the middle? The silence? The waiting that stretches into what feels like spiritual neglect?

That's where most of us are.

And that's where spiritual maturity happens. Because trusting God when He speaks is beautiful.

But trusting Him when He's *silent,* that's **intimacy**.

That's the moment you stop worshiping the feeling, and start worshiping the **faithfulness**.

Maybe just maybe, God Is Doing More in the Silence Than You Think

Maybe you don't hear Him because He's *sitting with you.* Not shouting orders. Just holding you.

Maybe the lesson isn't in the answer, it's in the **dependence**.

Maybe the silence is what teaches you how to stay, when staying feels hard.

God's silence isn't a wall.

It's often a **veil**; thin, sacred, painful; meant to draw you closer, not push you away.

He isn't hiding.

He's **inviting**.

Even now. Even here.

You're Still Safe Here

You are not drifting. You are not forgotten. You are not failing because you can't feel Him.

God sees the fight behind your stillness. He sees the effort it takes to keep hoping. He sees the tears you don't let fall because you're trying to be "strong."

He sees you when no one else does, and He's still near.

Even if He isn't saying much.

Sometimes the most intimate thing He can do... is simply stay silent and still love you.

Prayer:

> God,
> I don't know how to feel safe when You're quiet. I want to believe You're near. But honestly, it feels like I'm praying into the void. I've begged. I've waited. I've trusted with trembling hands. And still, I can't feel You. I can't hear You. And it hurts.
> Remind me that You're still here. That I don't have to hear Your voice to trust Your heart. That the silence doesn't mean I've been forgotten, it means You're drawing me into a deeper kind of faith. If You're doing something in me, I surrender to it.
> Even if it's quiet. Even if it's slow. Even if I never understand the "why." Just don't let me go. Even when I don't feel You, hold onto me. Anchor me in truth when emotions fail me.
> Let this silence make me softer, not harder. Let it make me holy, not bitter. Let it form something beautiful in me I couldn't get from clarity. Because at the end of the day... I still choose You. Even if You whisper. Even if You wait. You are still safe. You are still good. You are still mine.
> In Jesus' name,
> Amen.

Journal Prompt:

Where do I feel like God is silent right now?

What have I been afraid to say out loud to Him because I wasn't sure if He was listening?

What would I say if I truly believed His silence was not rejection, but invitation?

Day 16

SAFE WHEN YOU'RE CRUSHED

"The Lord is near to the brokenhearted, and saves those who are crushed in spirit."
Psalm 34:18

THERE'S A KIND OF pain that takes your breath away.

Not physically, but emotionally. Spiritually. It hits like a wave you didn't see coming. And suddenly you're lying awake at 2:00 a.m. staring at the ceiling, wondering how you're supposed to keep going.

Crushed in spirit.

That's the Bible's word for it.

It's not dramatic.

It's not weak.

It's **honest**.

It's the kind of sorrow that doesn't just break you; it folds you inward.

You forget how to ask for help.

You forget what peace felt like.

You forget how to breathe without clenching.

What do you do when the weight won't lift?

You pray.

You cry.

You do all the things people tell you to do.

And still; no breakthrough.

Still, no answers.

Still, no relief.

That's the kind of crushing this verse is talking about.

Not the frustration of a bad day.

But the devastation of a broken heart.

The kind of heartbreak that makes you question not just what happened; but *who you are now that it did.*

You start wondering: *"Did I do something wrong?" "Did God forget about me?" "Is there something defective in me that makes healing skip over me?"*

You Can't Fix Yourself; And You Don't Have To

The world tells you to bounce back.

To grind your way through the grief.

To glow-up and pretend nothing wrecked you.

But here's what Scripture says:

> *"The Lord is near to the brokenhearted and saves those who are crushed in spirit."*

He doesn't stand at a distance, waiting for you to pull it together.

He comes *close.*

Not after you recover.

Right there in the wreckage.

And He doesn't shame your crushing.

He calls it the place where He can do **His most intimate work.**

But, What If the Crushing is Sacred?

It doesn't feel like it, I know.

It feels like loss.

It feels like rejection.

It feels like failure.

But what if the crushing isn't punishment, what if it's **preparation?**

In Gethsemane, Jesus wasn't just praying, He was being crushed.

Literally.

"Gethsemane" means *oil press*; a place where olives are crushed to release what's hidden inside.

Jesus wasn't weak in that garden.

He was *yielded*.

And out of that surrender came salvation for the world.

Sometimes the pressing you feel isn't a sign you're being forgotten.

It's a sign that God is preparing to bring something sacred from your sorrow.

So Don't Rush the Rescue

We want out of pain fast.

But some things need time.

God doesn't waste your crushing.

He doesn't rush it.

He doesn't ask you to fake your way through it.

He meets you *in it*.

You may not feel strong; but you are *safe*.

You are *held*.

You are *seen*.

And even when you don't see Him move, He is still near.

Safety Doesn't Mean the Pain Stops; It Means You're Not Alone In It

This may not be the season of joy yet.

You may still be weeping.

Still wondering.

Still waking up with a lump in your chest that won't leave.

But hear this:

You are safe in the crushing.

Not because the pain goes away.

But because God is in the pain with you.

Holding your heart like it's His own, because it *is*.

Binding up the shattered pieces with mercy.

Kissing your forehead with presence.

Weeping when you weep, and refusing to let the darkness have the final word. You don't have to be okay right now.

You just have to be *here*.

With Him.

Let Him hold what you can't carry anymore.

Prayer:
God, I feel crushed.
Not just hurt, but undone. Not just shaken, but shattered. And honestly? I've tried to hold it together. To pray like I'm fine. To worship like I'm not aching. But I can't fake it with You. You already know.
So here I am.
No filter. No mask. No strength left. You said You're near to the brokenhearted. You said You save those who are crushed in spirit. So save me here, not by changing everything right away, but by reminding me that I'm not alone in it.
I need to feel Your nearness, Lord.
I don't need a miracle today, just a moment. A whisper that You're still with me. A breath of comfort that doesn't ask me to rush the healing. I lay my crushed places in Your hands. Do what only You can.
Make beauty out of brokenness.
Let this crushing become holy ground.
In Jesus' name,
Amen.

Journal Prompt:

Where do I feel crushed right now?

What grief or disappointment have I been trying to push down instead of placing in God's hands?

Can I trust Him to meet me in this space; not to rush me, but to hold me?

SAFE IN THE STRUGGLE TO FORGIVE

"Be kind to one another, compassionate, forgiving each other, just as God in Christ also has forgiven you." Ephesians 4:32

FORGIVENESS SOUNDS NOBLE UNTIL you actually have to do it.

Until it's not just a sermon note but someone's name in your mouth, and all the hurt comes rushing back.

Until it's not a theological concept but a face you see in your memories, in your nightmares, in the way you flinch when someone raises their voice or uses a certain tone.

Forgiveness isn't clean.

It's not pretty.

It's not a quick prayer and a quiet heart.

It's a struggle.

A deep, gut-wrenching, wrestling-with-God kind of surrender.

It doesn't mean you're weak. It means you're human. And it means you've been hurt.

Forgiveness Is Not Denial

Forgiveness doesn't say:

- "It didn't hurt."
- "It didn't change me."
- "They were right."
- "I'm fine now."

Forgiveness says:

"It was real. It was painful. It was wrong.

But I will not carry the poison of it in my soul any longer."

You are allowed to grieve the wound. You are allowed to feel the injustice.

You are allowed to sit with the ache before you release it. God doesn't demand you fake healing. He invites you to bring your cracked, calloused heart and say:

"Lord, I can't do this without You. But I want to be free."

Forgiveness Isn't Agreement; It's Release

You forgiving them doesn't mean what they did was okay.

It doesn't mean it didn't cost you something.

It doesn't mean they deserve trust, or access, or a second chance.

Forgiveness is not letting them off the hook.

It's letting **yourself** off the hook of bitterness, vengeance, and soul exhaustion.

It's refusing to keep bleeding for someone else's sin.

"Forgive... just as God in Christ also has forgiven you." — Ephesians 4:32

This verse doesn't say:

- "When they apologize."

- "When it stops hurting."

- "When justice is served."

It says *"just as Christ forgave you."*

Undeserved.

Freely.

Fully.

Not because you were innocent, but because He was **that merciful.**

But What About When It Still Hurts?

Let's not romanticize forgiveness.

Sometimes you forgive, and the pain stays.

Sometimes you forgive, and they hurt you again.

Sometimes you forgive, and they never know, never care, never change.

You're not broken because it's still hard.

You're not unholy because it still stings.

Forgiveness isn't always a one-time event.

Sometimes it's a daily choice.

Sometimes it's a **war;** where you wake up and say again:

"God, I choose to release them; not because they're worthy, but because I'm tired of being chained to what they did."

It's okay if it's not instant. It's okay if it's not beautiful. It's still holy.

Did you know...You're Safe to Forgive; Even if They Never Change

This is where it gets personal. You can forgive because you're **safe** in Jesus.

Not because your trust is in people, but because your anchor is in Him.

He is your vindication. He is your justice. He is your comfort. He is your safe place. The person who hurt you may never own what they did. They may still be manipulating, minimizing, avoiding.

But you?

You get to walk out of the prison cell and shut the door behind you. Because forgiveness is not permission for them; it's **freedom for you.**

What About the Ones Who Should've Protected You?

This is the hardest kind of forgiveness.

When the one who hurt you was supposed to *guard* you. When they were trusted. Respected. Maybe even *"anointed."* When they were the ones who should've said:

- "I believe you."
- "I see your pain."
- "You didn't deserve that."

But instead they blamed.

Dismissed.

Gaslit.

Covered it up.

You were wounded by someone you were told to revere. And now the weight of forgiveness feels unbearable.

Hear me:

God is not siding with your abuser. God is not asking you to rush your healing. God does not minimize your pain.

He is the God who *sees*.

He is the God who *knows*.

And He is the God who says:

> *"Justice is Mine. I will repay."* Romans 12:19

You can release your right to revenge; because God holds the gavel.

You can release them from your hands, because God never drops the case.

The Safety Isn't in the Outcome; It's in the Savior

You may never get the apology.

You may never see the restoration you hoped for.

You may never understand why they did what they did.

But you are **still safe.**

Because Jesus holds every shattered piece.

Because you are not defined by your pain—you are **redeemed** from it.

Because the cross was enough.

You don't forgive because you're over it.

You forgive because **Jesus overcame it.**

Prayer:
God, I want to forgive... but I don't know how. I've carried this pain for so long, it's almost part of me. I've replayed the memories. I've swallowed the bitterness. I've smiled through the ache just to survive. And still... it hurts.

So I bring You the truth: They hurt me. They changed me. They left me with wounds I didn't ask for. But I don't want to stay stuck here.

Jesus, teach me to forgive, not because they're worthy, but because *You* are. Help me release what I was never meant to carry. Help me lay down what's too heavy for my soul.

Help me trust that You see, You know, and You will make all things right. I don't have to pretend it didn't hurt. But I also don't have to let it hold me hostage. So I breathe deep and whisper:

I forgive.

Maybe not perfectly. Maybe not completely. But honestly. And with You. Do what I can't. Heal the part of me that still aches. And let my freedom begin now.

In Jesus' name,
Amen.

Journal Prompt:

Who have I struggled to forgive, and why?

What has that pain cost me?

What do I need to say to God today that I've been afraid to admit about that wound.? Write without censoring. Let it all out. Then ask Him to begin the work of healing, even if you're not ready to release it all yet.

Day 18

SAFE IN THE SORROW

"You have taken account of my miseries; Put my tears in Your bottle. Are they not in Your book?" Psalm 56:8

THERE ARE MOMENTS THAT split life in two.

Before.

And **after.**

Moments that don't feel like moments at all, but hurricanes of heartbreak, waves of devastation, silences that scream.

The Texas Flood of 2025 was one of those moments.

It wasn't just water.

It was the memory of everything being ripped away in minutes.

It was sirens and helicopters and streets that looked like rivers.

It was watching people cling to rooftops, to each other, to anything that still felt real. It was mothers carrying babies through chest-deep waters.

It was homes that would never be lived in again.

It was children asking questions with no soft answers.

It was pastors trying to preach peace with swollen eyes and shaking hands.

It was entire neighborhoods swallowed; and survivors wondering why they were the ones still standing.

This is Sorrow

This isn't inconvenience. This isn't discomfort. This is *loss*.

Sorrow doesn't knock. It kicks in the door and sits heavy on your chest.

It steals the words from your mouth and the light from your eyes.

And the hardest part? Sorrow doesn't ask if you're ready. It just comes.

Sometimes it wears the face of disaster.

Sometimes it comes with a phone call.

Sometimes it shows up in a memory that won't stop replaying.

But whatever form it takes; grief is not gentle. It's a thief, a fog, a scream you swallow while life keeps marching like nothing happened. And maybe, just maybe, that's the part that hurts most

You Want to Believe You're Safe. But This Doesn't Feel Like It

This wasn't supposed to happen. Not to your city. Not to your family. Not to your home. The foundation cracked. Not just in the streets; but in your soul.

You prayed.

You believed.

You stayed.

But the flood still came.

And now you're walking through the aftermath, mud on your boots and grief in your lungs.

You're told to "be strong," but what you really need is permission to **fall apart.**

Where Was God?

That's the question no one wants to say out loud.

But you've asked it a thousand times in the quiet:

"God, where were You when the waters rose?" "Where were You when my baby couldn't stop crying, and I didn't know what to do?" "Where were You when the roof caved in?" "Where were You when the people I loved didn't make it out?"

It feels heretical to ask; but He's not afraid of your questions.

Because He was there. Not as the cause, but as the *constant.*

He was in the neighbor who carried you.

In the stranger who prayed as your house disappeared.

In the rescuer who whispered, *"I've got you."*

In the shelter where hands passed out blankets with trembling grace.

And even when you couldn't see Him...

He was the One weeping with you in the rain.

Grief Is Not a Detour from Faith; It's a Road Jesus Knows

We often want faith to feel strong. Certain. Put together. But faith in grief?

It's a **whimper**. A desperate reach. A holy, hollow ache. Jesus wept at Lazarus's tomb. He *knew* resurrection was coming, but He still stopped and cried. Because presence doesn't skip pain.

It **sits in it.**

Your grief doesn't disqualify your belief.

Your sorrow doesn't cancel your safety.

You can scream into your pillow and still be held by the arms that formed the stars. You are still loved in the weeping. Still carried in the questions. Still safe; even here.

What Is Safe, When Everything's Gone?

Safe isn't the absence of storms.

It's the presence of the **One who speaks to them.** It's not always deliverance from the flood, but the hand that holds you *through* it.

He didn't promise to stop every wave.

He promised:

> *"When you pass through the waters, I will be with you."* — Isaiah 43:2

The sorrow is real.

But so is the Savior.

And even now, as you pick through the pieces, as you sit in borrowed clothes in makeshift shelters, as you grieve what can't be rebuilt, He is still your shelter.

Not the one made of bricks. But the one made of love that doesn't leave.

What If the Sorrow Isn't the End?

This isn't where your story stops.

You don't have to pretend you're okay.

But you also don't have to believe that this is forever.

You will carry this loss, yes.

But you are also carried.

By the One who knows every name lost.

By the One who records every tear you cry.

By the One who catches what the flood tried to steal, your faith, your hope, your identity; and tucks it into His heart until you're ready to hold it again.

The sorrow is sacred. But it is not eternal.

Hope Still Grows in Mud

You may not believe it yet.

But one day, the ground will dry. And when it does, you will find something buried in the wreckage:

resilience.

community.

faith with scars.

hope that knows how to hold pain.

You'll sit with someone else in their sorrow, and you'll whisper, *"I've been there. You're not alone."*

And you'll become proof that grief doesn't win. That floods don't get the final say. That God still speaks after the storm. And maybe, just maybe, that's how beauty rises from devastation.

Prayer:
God, I'm not okay. And I won't pretend to be. I've seen things I can't unsee.

Heard the cries I can't forget. Lost things I didn't think I could live without.

This flood didn't just take possessions; it took *peace.*

I don't know what to do with the weight of this sorrow. But I give You what's left of me. Be my shelter when the world breaks. Be my calm when my heart won't stop racing. Be the arms that hold me when everything else is gone.

You said You put my tears in a bottle. So I give You every one. Every "why." Every ache. Every night I didn't sleep. Every scream I couldn't voice.

Be near, God. Be loud, even if I can't hear You yet. Be kind to my broken places. Be patient when I'm angry. Be strong when I'm too weak to hope.

I don't need a miracle. I need You. Stay with me in the sorrow. And when the time comes; walk with me into healing.

In Jesus' name,
Amen.

Journal Prompt:

What have I lost that I haven't fully grieved yet?

Where does my sorrow feel too heavy to carry?

What would it look like to trust God with my heartbreak; not because I'm ready to move on, but because I can't hold it alone anymore?

SAFE WHEN YOU START TO REBUILD

"The Lord will continually lead you, And satisfy your desire in scorched places, And give strength to your bones; And you will be like a watered garden, And like a spring of water whose waters do not fail."
Isaiah 58:11

YOU'VE SURVIVED THE STORM.

But now comes the part no one prepares you for: **Starting over.**

It's quiet here—too quiet, maybe.

No headlines.

No hashtags.

No rescue boats.

Just rubble.

And you.

The adrenaline is gone.

The casseroles have stopped coming.

And you're staring at what's left of your life, wondering how to take the next step. No one talks about how sacred, how *terrifying*, how *holy* it is to rebuild.

You Don't Start with a Blueprint; You Start with Debris

The ground feels unfamiliar. What used to be home is now dust. What used to be "us" is now "used to be."

Rebuilding isn't glamorous. It's tears and paperwork. It's phone calls and flashbacks. It's cleaning out drawers filled with someone else's memories. It's asking questions like:

- *"Do I even want to start over?"*

- *"What if I fail again?"*

- *"Is it okay to be hopeful when I'm still hurting?"*

You're not being dramatic. You're being **human**. And the God who formed humanity from dust knows exactly what to do with a soul that's shattered.

Rebuilding Is More Than Recovery; It's Resurrection

This isn't just putting things back the way they were. That's not even possible Grief has changed you. Loss has shaped you. Sorrow has softened the edges that used to be sharp with self-sufficiency.

This time, you're not rebuilding for appearances. You're rebuilding with **presence**. You're not creating the life you used to have. You're receiving the life God is making *with you* now.

Resurrection doesn't mean returning. It means *rising*. In new ways. With new wisdom. With a limp maybe; but with the Lord.

Rebuilding Isn't Fast, It's Faithful

You'll want to hurry. You'll want to paint over pain with productivity.

You'll want to skip the process. You'll want to convince everyone (including yourself) that you're okay. But rushing recovery is just a slower collapse.

God isn't asking you to prove anything.

He's asking you to *trust* Him. Trust Him with the pieces. With the timeline. With the mess. With your pace.

If all you can do today is breathe and brush your teeth, you're still rebuilding.

Because survival was a miracle.

And recovery is a ministry.

You are a walking testimony already.

It's Okay to Be Afraid

Rebuilding brings up fear you didn't expect:

- *What if it falls apart again?*
- *What if I'm not strong enough?*
- *What if God doesn't show up this time?*

But hear this:

The God who met you in the flood will meet you in the framework.

He's not just the rescuer.

He's the restorer.

You don't have to carry this alone.

You don't have to pretend you're brave when you're still shaking.

You don't have to know what it'll look like—you just have to keep showing up.

You are not rebuilding **for** Him.

You are rebuilding **with** Him.

Sometimes All You Can Do Is Lay a Brick

There will be days the pain still hits like a wave.

Days when your hands tremble at the weight of starting over.

Days when you look around and wonder if you're really up to the task.

You don't have to build a house in a day.

Some days, the holy work is just **laying one brick.**

- Call a counselor.
- Sort a drawer.
- Say a prayer through gritted teeth.
- Read a verse and cry through it.
- Say yes to coffee with a friend.

Every tiny act of faith is a brick in the sacred architecture of your healing.

Safe Doesn't Mean It's Easy

Safe doesn't mean painless. Safe means **you're not alone** in it.

It means Jesus is in the ruins, helping you pick up what's still worth keeping.

It means the Holy Spirit is your strength when you're too tired to try again.

It means your foundation isn't the past; it's the promise that God *never* wastes a life willing to rise again.

You're not being foolish by hoping. You're being *faithful.*

You Are Becoming Something Beautiful

Isaiah says you will be "like a watered garden." That doesn't happen in a day. It happens seed by seed. Watered by tears. Grown through storms. But make no mistake: This rebuilding is not just recovery.

It's **revival**.

And the world needs to see what God can do with a life that refused to give up in the dark.

Prayer:
God, I don't know how to start over.
I'm standing in the middle of what's left,
and everything feels too fragile, too broken, too painful to move.
I'm tired. I'm scared. And I don't want to pretend I'm strong.
But I trust that You are.
So today, I give You what I have:
One broken heart.
Two trembling hands.
And a soul willing to try.
Help me rebuild with You.
Not out of pressure, but out of promise.
Not out of shame, but out of surrender.
Not out of fear, but with fire in my bones.
Be the architect of my healing.
Be the foundation I lay my hope on.
Be the strength when my faith falters.
Be the joy that finds me even here
I don't need to have it all figured out.
I just need to know You're with me.
And You are. So brick by brick I'll rise.
In Jesus' name,
Amen.

Journal Prompt:

What part of rebuilding feels the scariest to me right now?

What am I holding onto that God might be asking me to lay down?

What could it look like to trust Him with one small step today?

SAFE WHEN YOU'RE THE STRONG ONE

"Come to Me, all who are weary and burdened, and I will give you rest. Take My yoke upon you and learn from Me, for I am gentle and humble in heart, and you will find rest for your souls." Matthew 11:28–29

YOU'RE THE ONE THEY call when things fall apart.

You're the emergency contact, the fixer, the calm in the chaos.

You're the "prayer warrior," the "mama bear," the dependable one.

You don't fall apart in public.

You handle things. You make the plan. You carry the weight.

You're the strong one.

And if you're honest?

You're tired.

But who do you tell that to when everyone depends on your strength?

Where do you go when you're the one everyone leans on?

Strength is a gift.

But it can become a cage.

Because being strong doesn't always feel safe.

Sometimes it feels like pressure.

Sometimes it feels like isolation.

Sometimes it feels like slowly unraveling while saying, *"I'm fine."*

And the scary thing?

You've worn that strength so long, you're not sure who you are without it.

You know how to:

1. Carry the groceries, the grief, and the group chat.

2. Keep showing up, even with a broken heart.

3. Encourage others while your soul is exhausted.

4. Hold space for everyone else while your own space is cracking.

But have you ever wondered if God meant for you to carry it all?

Who's Carrying You?

Jesus didn't say, "Come to Me, all who have it together."

He said: *"Come to Me, all who are weary and burdened, and I will give you rest."* Matthew 11:28

But strong people don't always feel like they can admit they're weary.

They're afraid the whole world might fall apart if they do.

Here's the truth:

You can still be strong and need rest.

You can still be faithful and feel fragile.

You can still be a leader and long to be held.

You were never designed to be everyone's Savior.

That position is already taken.

Your Strength Is Not Your Worth

Somewhere along the line, maybe you believed a lie: That being "the strong one" makes you worthy.

That holding it together earns you love. That if you stop carrying everything, people will leave.

But you are not loved because you're strong.

You are loved because you're His.

Not for what you do.

Not for what you fix.

Not for what you carry.

Just for being His child.

Messy. Tired. Human.

He doesn't love your mask.

He loves *you*.

Hard truth...Even Strong People Break

And you should know this: Jesus doesn't flinch when you finally collapse.

He doesn't shame your breakdown.

He doesn't roll His eyes when your strong exterior finally cracks.

He kneels next to you, whispers peace over your shaking shoulders,

and says, *"I've been here the whole time."*

You are not disappointing God by needing Him.

You are not weak for finally saying, *"I can't do this anymore."*

You are safe to fall apart in His presence.

Safe to be honest.

Safe to need.

Lay Down What Was Never Yours to Carry

You've picked up so many things.

Their grief.

Their expectations.

Their emergency after emergency. Their survival.

But let's ask something holy and hard:

What of that did God actually ask you to carry?

You can be compassionate *without* being crushed.

You can help *without* handing over your peace.

You can love people deeply *without* losing yourself.

There is strength in **surrender.**

In admitting you need help.

In asking God to carry what you can't.

There's nothing wrong with being the strong one.

But even strong ones need somewhere to lay their head.

Let that place be Jesus.

I'm gonna hold your hand when i say this... A Gentle Warning

Sometimes "strong" becomes a performance. You show up. Smile. Serve.

And inside? You're slowly disappearing.

You've become everyone's rock, and no one knows you're drowning.

You don't have to keep pretending.

The Savior of the world has no interest in your performance.

He wants your presence.

He wants you. Even if you come to Him empty-handed, burned out, and barely holding it together.

<u>You're enough.</u>

<u>Right here.</u>

<u>Right now.</u>

You don't have to earn your rest. God isn't asking for more hustle, He's offering **healing**.

What if strength today looks like:

Saying no.

Going to therapy.

Turning off your phone.

Crying without apology.

Asking for help.

Taking a nap.

Letting someone take care of *you* for once.

You are not the glue holding everyone together.

God is. Let Him hold *you* too.

Prayer:
Jesus, I'm tired.
Not the kind of tired sleep can fix. The kind of tired that lives in my bones. The kind I've hidden for too long. I've been the strong one. The capable one. The "don't worry about me" one.
But I'm breaking. And I don't know how to stop holding it all. So here it is, God: All the things I've carried. All the pressure I've worn like a badge. All the pain I've swallowed with a smile. I lay it down. At Your feet. In Your arms. I don't want to be everyone's savior.
I just want to be wholly Yours.
Be my strength when mine runs out. Be my peace when the world pulls at me. Be the one who carries *me*. Because I'm done pretending.
I need You. I trust You. And I know You'll never drop what I put in Your hands.
Thank You for being safe, even for the strong ones.
In Jesus' name,
Amen.

Journal Prompt:

What am I carrying that God never asked me to?

Why do I feel pressure to be "the strong one"?

What would it look like to be held, instead of holding everyone else?

SAFE IN SUCCESS

"Every good thing given and every perfect gift is from above, coming down from the Father of lights, with whom there is no variation or shifting shadow." James 1:17

SUCCESS IS A STRANGE kind of storm.

From the outside, it looks like sunshine.

The job promotion. The book deal. The growing business. The ministry impact. The healthy bank account. The "answered prayer" moment.

People clap for you.

They congratulate you.

They post about you.

And you smile, because you *are* grateful. You know this is a blessing. But here's the thing no one tells you about success:

It can be just as disorienting as failure.

When you've prayed for something and it finally happens, you expect to feel free.

But success often comes with invisible chains:

"What if I can't keep this up?"

"What if I lose it?"

"What if I'm not actually good enough to deserve this?"

"What if they realize I'm just figuring it out as I go?"

The higher you climb, the more visible the fall.

And sometimes, instead of resting in the blessing, you start hustling harder to prove you belong at the table God already set for you.

Success can be isolating.

Some people pull away because they're jealous.

Others start treating you differently, like you're less human and more of a symbol.

And some expect you to keep producing, keep winning, keep achieving at all costs.

The applause fades, and you're left with questions:

"Who can I be real with now?"

"Who loves me for me, not for what I can do?"

"If I slow down, will I still matter?"

It's possible to be surrounded by people and still feel completely alone; especially when you're known for your wins, but not your wounds.

Remember: The Gift is Not the God

James 1:17 reminds us that *every good thing comes from the Father.*

That means the success you're standing in right now isn't just the result of your grind, it's a gift from God.

But here's where it gets dangerous:

We can start worshiping the gift instead of the Giver.

We protect the platform more than the Presence.

We guard the image more than the intimacy.

And when we start defining ourselves by what we've achieved instead of *whose we are*, we step into a very fragile kind of living. Because if your identity is built on what you've built, what happens when it's gone?

Safe in the Spotlight

God never intended for success to become a source of anxiety.

He meant it to be a *testimony,* a way for the world to see His faithfulness.

That means:

- You don't have to keep proving your worth.

- You don't have to outdo yourself every year.

- You don't have to pretend everything is perfect when you're struggling.

You are safe to succeed without selling your soul.

Safe to celebrate without carrying the crushing weight of "what's next?"

Safe to rest, yes, even when the world says, *"Keep going or you'll lose momentum."*

Success Without Surrender is Still Empty

We live in a culture obsessed with the next milestone.

But God is not pacing heaven, stressed out about your growth metrics, your follower count, or your quarterly performance.

He's after your heart.

If success costs you peace with God, it's not really success.

If it costs you your family, your integrity, your health—it's not a blessing anymore. Success without surrender is just noise.

But success surrendered to God becomes a song.

How to Stay Grounded When You're Winning

1. Stay in the Word.

Let Scripture be louder than the applause or the criticism.

Success can blur your vision, truth clears it.

2. Keep trusted people close.

People who can call you out and pray you through.

People who loved you before the title, the income, or the platform.

3. Remember your Source.

Say it out loud: *"God gave me this. God sustains this. God can redirect this."*

4. Rest intentionally.

Don't wait until burnout forces you to stop. Sabbath is for the successful, too.

5. Give it away.

Your success is a resource for the Kingdom, not just a reward for you.

The Safety Net of Success

You're safe in success, not because the blessing can't be taken away, but because **God can't be.**

If the deal falls through, He's still your provider.

If the followers unfollow, He's still your audience of One.

If the season changes, He's still your steady ground.

The true safety in success isn't in keeping it.

It's in knowing your soul is held whether you have it or not.

Prayer:
God, I thank You for every good thing You've given me. I know I didn't get here on my own. I know my success is not just hard work, it's Your faithfulness. And I don't want to lose sight of that.

Protect my heart from pride. Protect my mind from fear. Protect my spirit from chasing the gift more than the Giver. Remind me that I'm loved, not for what I do, but for who I am in You. Remind me that if it's gone tomorrow, I'm still secure in Your hands. Teach me to steward this season well. To rest when I need to. To celebrate without worshiping the success. To keep my eyes on You in the spotlight. Because the only win that matters is finishing this life faithful to You.

In Jesus' name,
Amen.

Journal Prompt:

What fears have surfaced now that I've achieved something I prayed for?

Am I finding my identity in the blessing or in the One who gave it?

What boundaries do I need to put in place to protect my heart in this season?

SAFE WHEN YOU LOSE IT ALL

"The Lord gives and the Lord takes away. Blessed be the name of the Lord." Job 1:21b

LOSS DOESN'T ALWAYS KNOCK first.

Sometimes it just walks in and empties the room.

The phone rings. The market crashes. The diagnosis drops. The relationship ends. The storm hits. The call you prayed would come… doesn't.

And suddenly, you're standing in the ruins of what used to be, wondering how you're supposed to keep breathing when everything you built, loved, or counted on is gone.

When the Bottom Falls Out

There's a silence after loss that feels louder than any noise.

The way the air feels heavy.

The way your body aches with grief.

The way you stare at the same wall for an hour because your mind can't move past what just happened.

People try to comfort you:

- "God has a plan."
- "You'll come back stronger."
- "At least you still have ____."

And maybe those things are true.

But right now, they don't touch the hollow in your chest.

Because what you've lost isn't just a thing.

It's a life you'll never get back.

It's dreams you buried in the rubble.

It's a chapter that slammed shut while you were still reading it.

Job Knew This Pain

Job didn't lose a *little*.

He lost *everything*; wealth, health, children, reputation, in what felt like the span of a breath.

And yet, his first response wasn't denial.

It was grief.

Scripture says he tore his robe, shaved his head, and fell to the ground.

That's important.

Job didn't skip mourning.

He didn't call it "fine" or put a positive spin on it.

But in the middle of that devastation, he still whispered:

"The Lord gives and the Lord takes away. Blessed be the name of the Lord."

This wasn't toxic positivity.

This was surrender to the only truth that couldn't be taken from him: **God is still God.**

Safe Doesn't Mean You Keep Everything

We often define safety as holding onto what we love.

But biblical safety is deeper, it's knowing **you are held even when you lose what you love.**

It's the kind of safety that says:

- Even if the account is empty, God is still my provider.
- Even if my body fails, He's still my healer.
- Even if relationships walk away, He's still the One who stays.

God never promised we wouldn't lose things.

He promised we'd never lose *Him*.

When You Lose More Than You Thought You Could Bear

Maybe your loss was expected but still crushed you.

Maybe it blindsided you so hard you still can't catch your breath.

Maybe you've lost so much, you're not sure there's anything left to take.

I want you to hear me:

You are allowed to grieve this.

You are allowed to cry, collapse, question.

God is not impatient with your heartbreak.

He's not telling you to "get over it."

He's sitting in the ashes with you.

This isn't a season to perform.

It's a season to be *held*.

What If This Is Where the Real Foundation Shows?

Loss has a way of revealing where we've placed our trust.

It's not wrong to love what God has given.

But when it's gone, we're left with the question:

"Was my faith in the gift or the Giver?"

That's not a condemnation.

It's an invitation.

To rebuild on a foundation that can't be shaken.

To anchor to the One who isn't dependent on circumstances to keep His promises.

Everything else can shift.

God stays.

There's Still a Future After This

It doesn't feel like it right now.

Right now it feels like survival is the only goal.

And that's okay, sometimes surviving *is* the miracle.

But this isn't the end.

The God who restores double to Job, who raises dead things, who redeems shattered stories, is still writing yours.

Your loss is part of your story.

It is not the whole story.

Prayer:
God, I didn't want to lose this.
I prayed You'd protect it. I prayed You'd fix it. But here I am, standing in the empty space where it used to be. And I don't know how to move forward.
I'm not ready for "lessons." I'm not ready for "purpose." I just need You. Hold me here. Sit with me in the silence. Remind me that safety isn't about keeping everything, it's about never being without You.
I don't know what's next. I don't know how long this will hurt. But I know You are still here.
And for now, that's all I can hold onto.

In Jesus' name,
Amen.

Journal Prompt:

What have I lost that still feels too heavy to talk about with God?

How has this loss affected the way I see Him?

What would it look like to trust Him to hold me in this grief, without rushing me through it?

SAFE IN THE SECRET STRUGGLES

"Therefore, confess your sins to one another, and pray for one another so that you may be healed. A prayer of a righteous person, when it is brought about, can accomplish much." James 5:16

THERE ARE THINGS ABOUT you nobody knows.

Not because they're small.

But because they're *heavy*.

Because they would change the way people look at you.

Because saying them out loud feels like handing someone a loaded weapon they could use against you.

Some are things you've done. Some are things done to you. Some are temptations you fight daily. Some are patterns you thought you'd outgrow but haven't.

They live in the shadows.

And you've convinced yourself: "It's better this way. Safer this way. Hidden is safe."

But the truth?

Hiding is exhausting.

The Lonely Weight of a Secret

Secrets demand energy.

You have to manage the story.

Filter conversations.

Edit yourself so no one catches on.

And somewhere along the way, the secret stops being *what happened,*

it becomes *who you think you are.*

That's how shame works.

It doesn't just accuse you of doing something wrong.

It convinces you **you are wrong**.

Unworthy. Disqualified. Dirty.

And so you keep the mask on.

You show up at work.

You serve at church.

You post the verses.

And all the while, there's a war inside your head that no one sees.

God Already Knows..And Still Stays

This is where we have to go slow.

Because maybe part of you *knows* God sees it all... but the thought of Him looking too closely terrifies you.

You imagine His gaze like a spotlight; cold, harsh, exposing.

But Scripture says His eyes are like **fire** (Revelation 1:14). Not fire that destroys you, fire that *burns away the chains.*

He's not surprised by your struggle.

He's not discovering this for the first time.

And He's not walking away.

You can't scare Him off with the truth.

He already knows the truth, and loves you still.

The Difference Between a Secret and a Sacred Wound

Not every unspoken thing is meant for public consumption.

Some wounds are sacred, tender, still healing.

But there's a difference between keeping something sacred and keeping it *secret* out of fear.

Sacred wounds are tended to in the presence of God and safe people.

Secrets are left to rot in the dark. And the enemy thrives in the dark.

That's why bringing your struggle into the light, whether it's an addiction, an affair, a bitterness, a past abortion, a private doubt, isn't about humiliation.

It's about healing.

Confession Isn't Punishment, It's a Doorway

James 5:16 says: "Confess your sins to one another... so that you may be healed."

Confession isn't God trying to embarrass you.

It's Him trying to free you.

Because as long as you keep it in, the struggle owns you.

The second you bring it into the light, the power shifts.

The enemy loses his grip.

This is why the safest place to confess is to God first, and then to someone who knows how to handle fragile things without breaking them further.

Your Past Is Not Your Prison

Some of you reading this aren't trapped in a current struggle, you're trapped in a *memory*. Something you did years ago still haunts you.

It comes back when you're quiet.

It flares up when you're about to step into something new:

"Remember what you did? You're not the kind of person God uses."

Hear me:

If the blood of Jesus is enough to cleanse murderers, adulterers, deniers, betrayers, and Scripture is full of them; then it's enough for you, too.

That thing in your past?

It's not too big for the cross.

It's not too ugly for grace.

It's not the end of your story.

You Are Safe to Struggle

Being safe in God doesn't mean you're free from struggle.

It means you're free to be honest about it without fear of abandonment.

You're safe to say:

- "I'm still tempted."
- "I still slip sometimes."
- "I don't know why I can't shake this."
- "I'm afraid to tell anyone, but I need help."

You're safe to bring your struggle into prayer before it becomes a collapse.

You're safe to cry to Him in the middle of the night instead of cleaning yourself up for the morning.

You're safe to confess without being condemned.

The First Step Out of Hiding

Maybe your first step isn't telling a friend yet.

Maybe it's telling God.

Out loud. Unedited.

And maybe your second step is asking Him for one safe person to help you carry this.

Don't overcomplicate it.

Don't overthink it.

Light kills shame.

Every time.

This is "The Beauty of Being Fully Known"

The irony of hiding is that you ache to be known.

But you're terrified of what knowing might cost you.

Here's the truth:

Being *fully* known, by God, by even one safe person, and still loved is the most healing experience on earth.

You'll find that when love meets your worst, something breaks loose inside you.

You breathe deeper.

You walk lighter.

And the struggle you thought defined you begins to lose its name.

Prayer:
God, I've been hiding.
From You. From others. Sometimes even from myself.
I've carried things I was never meant to carry alone.
I've kept silent because I was afraid of judgment.
Afraid of rejection. Afraid of being truly seen.
But You see me already.
And You still call me Yours. So here it is, my struggle.
My past. My temptation. My regret. All of it. I put it in Your hands because I know You won't crush me. You'll cover me. You'll cleanse me. You'll heal me. Show me who I can trust to walk with me in this. Help me reject the lie that I am my worst moment. And remind me that the cross is big enough, strong enough, final enough to cover even this. Thank You that I am safe, even in the places I've never dared to speak of.
In Jesus' name,
Amen.

Journal Prompt:

What am I hiding from God, even though He already knows?

Is my secret a sacred wound that needs time, or a shame wound that needs light?

Who could be a safe, God-honoring person to share this with?

SAFE WHEN YOU'RE ANGRY WITH GOD

"Be angry, and yet do not sin; do not let the sun go down on your anger." Ephesians 4:26 NASB

THERE'S A KIND OF silence we learn to sit in when we're angry with God.

It's not always loud.

It doesn't always scream.

Sometimes it just withdraws. Goes quiet. Shuts off the worship playlist. Stops praying, not out of unbelief but out of exhaustion and confusion.

No one wants to admit it, but sometimes, the people who love God the most are also the ones carrying the heaviest grief and the loudest questions.

And it is possible to be *furious* and *faithful* at the same time.

Maybe you've been there.

Or maybe you're there right now.

Where the prayers feel hollow.

Where "trust God" sounds like salt in the wound.

Where you're not sure if you're holding onto Him, or if you're just afraid to let go because you've been taught that letting go would mean spiritual failure.

Let me say this, loud and clear:

You are not a bad Christian for feeling angry.

Even Jesus, on the cross, cried out:

"My God, My God, why have You forsaken Me?" (Matthew 27:46 NASB)

Those were not calm, quiet words. They were screamed from lungs collapsing under the weight of injustice, abandonment, suffering.

If Jesus; the Son of God; could cry out in confusion and still be holy,

then so can you.

The Anger No One Sees

Some anger with God comes from deep, raw grief.

From loss you didn't see coming.

From prayers that went unanswered.

From betrayal by people who claimed to speak for Him.

From the ache of asking, *"If You could have stepped in... why didn't You?"*

This kind of anger is sacred ground.

It's not rebellion. It's heartbreak.

God is not threatened by it.

What if the real sin is not being angry... but pretending we aren't?

What if the most healing thing you could do right now is stop hiding your disappointment behind fake praise and let your Father meet you in the wreckage?

What Scripture Actually Says About Your Rage

We've been taught to tame ourselves.

To sit quietly in pews and say "God is good all the time" with a fake smile and clenched fists.

But the Bible is **not** full of tame people.

David raged.

Job yelled.

Jeremiah said he wished he had never been born.

Elijah laid down and begged to die.

Habakkuk basically screamed "WHERE ARE YOU?" into the wilderness.

And none of them got smited for it. Why?

Because **God never demands perfection of emotion. He invites honesty.**

"Come now, and let us debate your case," Says the Lord, "Though your sins are as scarlet, They shall become as white as snow.", Isaiah 1:18 NASB

He's not looking for sanitized, filtered feelings. He's looking for *you,* all of you.

Even the ugly parts. Especially the ugly parts. (especially those)

What to Do With the Fire Inside You

If you are in a season of fury with God, I want to offer you permission:

You don't have to fix it today. But you do have to bring it to Him.

Not your cleaned-up version of it.

Not the nice, socially acceptable prayer.

But the real cry of your heart.

Shout in your car.

Weep on the floor.

Write Him a letter.

Rip up a journal page.

Then wait. Not for immediate answers, maybe. But for Presence.

He won't leave you there.

He never has.

"The Lord is near to the brokenhearted And saves those who are crushed in spirit." Psalm 34:18 NASB

When You Feel Guilty for Feeling

Here's something the enemy doesn't want you to realize:

Shame is not a fruit of the Spirit.

Guilt over your honesty will not heal you faster.

And suppressing your anger doesn't make you righteous—it makes you resentful.

Letting God into your pain doesn't mean your faith is weak.

It means it's real.

It means you still believe He's there.

It means you trust Him enough to wrestle.

The Invitation in the Fire

Being safe in your anger with God doesn't mean you stay angry forever.

It means your anger doesn't have to be a wedge between you.

It can be a doorway.

Jacob wrestled with God all night and walked away with a limp.

But he also walked away with a blessing.

Don't fear the limp.

Some of the most sacred encounters with God happen when you stop pretending and just *wrestle it out with Him in the dirt.*

Because when the fire settles and your rage has burned down to embers,

you may just find He was sitting there with you the whole time.

Still holding you.

Still calling you His.

Still sheltering you, even when you screamed.

Prayer: A Cry From the Fire
God, I'm angry.
Not because I don't believe in You, but because I do. And I know You could have stepped in. You could have stopped it. But You didn't. And I don't understand why.
I don't want to fake it anymore. I don't want to pretend I'm fine when I'm falling apart inside. I bring You my questions. My frustration. My silence. My distance. I lay it at Your feet and I ask You to still love me here.
Don't let this anger harden me.
Let it break me open in a way that makes room for Your healing.
Sit with me in this fire, Father.
I don't need You to rush me, I just need You to stay.
Thank You that I'm still safe with You even in this. Even when I'm shouting. Even when I'm quiet. Even when I don't know what to pray.
Thank You for Your patience, Your tenderness, Your unrelenting presence.
Make me whole again. Even if it takes time. Even if I limp forever. Even if all I can say right now is "I'm still here."
In Jesus' name,
Amen.

Journal Prompts:

Has there ever been a moment in your life when you felt like God let you down?

What happened, and how did you respond? Did you shut down, pretend, or withdraw?

What would it look like to re-open that place with Him today?

SAFE WHEN YOU DOUBT YOUR FAITH

"Immediately the boy's father cried out and said, 'I do believe; help my unbelief!'"
Mark 9:24 NASB

YOU CAN LOVE GOD and still have questions.

You can follow Jesus and still feel lost.

You can raise your hands in worship and still wrestle with whether He hears your prayers.

Doubt isn't proof that you've lost your faith. Sometimes, it's the very evidence that you're still in the ring, still swinging, still trying to believe when nothing makes sense.

But if you've ever laid awake at night and thought, *What if none of this is real? What if I'm talking to the ceiling? What if God forgot about me?*

I want to tell you this:

You are not alone. And you are not disqualified.

When Faith Feels Fragile

You weren't supposed to be here, at least that's what they told you. "If you just have faith..." "If you just read more, pray more, fast more..." But here you are. Tired. Uncertain. Disoriented. Drowning in Doubt.

Maybe you used to feel God so clearly. Maybe you used to believe with boldness. Maybe you've seen miracles, lived through breakthroughs, experienced closeness with Him so real it made your bones feel warm.

But now?

Now the heavens feel closed.

Now the Word feels dry.

Now the prayers feel like they're bouncing off the ceiling.

You didn't choose doubt.

You woke up in it.

And you're scared to say it out loud because the last time you did, someone handed you a cliché or questioned your salvation.

But I won't do that.

Because I know what it's like to stare at your Bible, heartbroken, and whisper, *Are You even real?*

I know what it's like to be drowning in grief and get silence in return.

I know what it's like to beg for something to change, and watch everything fall apart instead.

Doubt Isn't the End

The enemy wants you to believe that doubt is the exit door of your faith.

But what if it's just a hallway? A hallway with doors on both sides. One leads deeper into the questions, the distance, the detachment. The other leads back into the arms of God, not with perfect understanding, but with surrendered trust.

Faith isn't pretending you don't struggle.

It's dragging your questions into the presence of God anyway. Despite your struggles, because of your questions...

Even the Saints Doubted

Abraham doubted the promise.

Moses doubted his ability.

David doubted God's timing.

Job doubted God's justice.

John the Baptist doubted Jesus' identity, even after proclaiming Him.

And Thomas? We still call him "Doubting Thomas" like it was his full name. But Jesus didn't shame him. Jesus showed him His scars.

That's what love does. It invites you closer when you're uncertain.

Jesus isn't threatened by your questions. He's not mad at your wrestling. He just doesn't want you to wrestle alone.

When Theology Collides With Reality

It's one thing to say "God is good." To sing of the "Goodness of God".

It's another thing to believe it when you're standing over a fresh grave.

Or sitting in a courtroom. Or holding a diagnosis. Or watching a loved one spiral.

Sometimes your theology crashes into your real life and all the pieces fall on the floor. And it feels like you're failing.

But you're not failing. You're growing.

Because what if God isn't trying to keep you in line, what if He's inviting you deeper? To a faith that isn't built on easy answers, but on intimate knowing.

What if you're not losing your faith? What if He's rebuilding it?

I think we forget that faith is not a one-time event. It isn't a just something that happened last week, last year.. last month. It's progressive and continuous, ever evolving and growing, and He reminds us of that through the word. Hebrews 11:1 "Now faith is... ", Romans 1:17 "For in it the righteousness of God is revealed from faith to faith..

Belief Isn't Always Loud

You don't have to shout to still believe.

Sometimes belief is whispering "help" with tears in your eyes.

Sometimes belief is opening your Bible even when it feels dry.

Sometimes belief is coming to church when everything in you wants to hide.

Sometimes belief is sitting in silence and saying, "God, I'm here. That's all I've got."

And guess what? That's enough.

Because God isn't grading you on the volume of your faith, i mean if He was.. mustard seeds would not move mountains. He's looking at your heart.

He sees the shaky hands, the bruised knees, the hoarse prayers, and He still calls it worship, but more than this.. He still calls it.

Safe to Stay

You're safe to stay, even when you don't understand.

You're safe to question, even when you don't feel qualified.

You're safe to weep, even when the answers don't come.

Faith isn't the absence of doubt. It's the decision to keep walking when you're not sure how it ends.

You are not a lost cause. You are not a disappointment. You are not too far gone.

You are loved right here. Seen right here. Held right here.

You are safe to doubt with the One who holds every answer, even when He's quiet.

Prayer: For the One Who's Not Sure Anymore
Jesus, I don't even know what to say. I feel like I'm losing something I once held tightly. Faith used to come easy. But now it feels fragile. Faint. Like a thread I'm barely hanging onto.
I want to believe You. I want to trust You. But I feel disconnected. I feel like You're far. And I'm scared to say it out loud because I don't want to be labeled or judged or told to "just pray more."
But You already know. So I'm saying it here.
Help my unbelief.
Help me feel You again.
Help me see past what I don't understand.
Don't let me go, even when I stop reaching.
Don't give up on me, even when I want to give up on You.
I need You more than ever. And even if I have nothing else, I give You this: I'm still here.
Meet me in the questions.
Hold me in the silence.
Anchor me in Your truth, even when I can't feel it.
I believe.
And I need You to carry the rest of me.
In Your mercy,
Amen.

Journal Prompt:

When did doubt first creek into your faith story? Was it after a loss, during a dry season, because of unanswered prayers, or slow disillusionment?

What does it mean to you to have faith and doubt at the same time? how does that tension stretch you, and how can it draw you closer to truth instead of further away?

Write a prayer or journal entry titles "Help My Unbelief." Let your words be honest, unfinished, and real. Don't edit it for God, He already knows.

SAFE WHEN YOU'RE TEMPTED TO NUMB OUT

"All things are permitted for me, but not all things are of benefit. All things are permitted for me, but I will not be mastered by anything." 1 Corinthians 6:12 NASB

LET'S GET HONEST.

There are moments in life when the pain is just too much. Not loud. Not dramatic. Just constant. Unrelenting. Exhausting. It lingers like background noise, humming behind your smile, behind the prayer hands emoji, behind the "I'm good, just tired." But deep down, you know. You're not okay. And the truth is, you haven't been okay for a while.

You used to feel it. The ache, the weight, the disappointment. But now?

You just scroll

Or binge.

Or pour.

Or eat.

Or shop.

Or obsessively plan every hour of your day because stillness feels like death.

It's not rebellion. It's not weakness. It's self-preservation. It's survival. And it's happening to people who love Jesus. People like you. People like me.

Let me say this plainly. You are not bad for wanting to escape.

You are human.

And God is not surprised by the ways you've tried to cope. But He does want to heal the part of you that feels like you have to disappear to survive. The part that says "self destruct mode" activated.

What Nobody Sees

Some of us weren't taught how to feel. We were taught how to function.

We were handed Bible verses like Band-Aids and told to press on. Be strong. Don't cry. Just trust God. So we did. But we learned to suppress instead of surrender. To hide instead of heal. We built systems in our souls. Escape routes. Emergency exits.

And now we're just... numb.

We can nod through sermons and cry at the chorus of worship songs, but the truth is we haven't felt close to God in months. Maybe longer. We're still showing up, but inside we've checked out. Not because we don't care. But because it hurts too much to care.

So we reach for what comforts in the moment. A glass. A pill. A plate. A scroll. A purchase. A mood. A person. Anything to not feel what we're feeling.

But here's the thing.

Numbing works until it doesn't.

It soothes, but it <u>NEVER</u> saves.

It dulls the ache, but it also quiets your soul's ability to hear the voice of the One who wants to heal you for real.

The Illusion of Control

We numb because it gives the illusion that we're still in control.

I'll only have one glass. I'll just check Instagram for five minutes. I'll just stay busy. I'll deal with this later.

But later never comes. And now you've built a habit. A go-to. A pacifier. And it doesn't look like a full-blown addiction, but it has mastered you.

The worst part?

You're not even sure if you want to give it up. Because it feels safe.

But friend, **the things we run to for safety are often the very things keeping us from being truly safe.**

A Soft Place to Land

Here's what you need to know.

You are not a failure for being overwhelmed. You are not weak for wanting to disconnect. You are not broken beyond repair.

God is not waiting for you to detox from your habits before He meets you in the middle.

He already sees the tabs you've left open.

He already hears the bag of chips rustling in your lap when you're crying on the floor.

He already knows the playlist you turn on when you don't want to feel anything.

And He still draws near.

Not to shame you. Not to fix you. Not to demand better behavior.

He comes close to **hold the part of you that has been holding your breath for years**.

What You Run From Will Eventually Rule You

The longer you run from the pain, the louder it will scream.

That's why numbing isn't a neutral act. It's a slow bleed.

You lose moments. You lose presence. You lose joy.

And you don't even realize it until you can't remember the last time you laughed without trying or prayed without guilt.

God doesn't want to just take away your coping mechanism. He wants to give you something better.

Peace that lasts.

Joy that's not tied to your circumstances.

Rest that doesn't come with a crash.

He wants to teach your nervous system to calm down in His presence.

He wants to sit with you in silence and help you realize you don't have to earn being held.

He wants to make your body feel like a safe place to live again.

It Starts With a Pause

Not a full surrender. Not a massive overhaul. Just one pause.

The next time you want to reach for the thing that numbs you, take 10 seconds.

Breathe.

Say His name.

Even whisper it if that's all you've got: "Jesus."

That moment is holy.

That pause is sacred.

And it breaks the power of the pattern.

Little by little, those seconds turn into minutes. Those minutes turn into connection. That connection turns into freedom.

And freedom always feels risky before it feels safe.

Prayer: For the One Who Can't Feel Anymore

God, I don't even know how I got here. I just know I've been surviving for so long that I forgot what it means to feel fully alive. I've been using things to comfort me. Maybe people. Maybe food. Maybe my phone. Maybe chaos itself. And I don't even know if I want to let it go. But I want to want to.

I'm tired of running. Tired of escaping. Tired of calling it peace when it's really just emotional shutdown. I bring You the truth. The real truth. The "I'm not okay" truth. I don't need You to scold me. I need You to sit with me.

I need You to hold the fear I've been avoiding. The memories I've stuffed down. The loneliness I've buried under busyness. The ache I've numbed. Teach me to stay. Not in pain forever, but in presence. Yours. Mine. Make me soft again. Make me feel again. Make me whole again.

Even if it's slow. Even if it's messy. Even if I cry more than I pray right now. I want You more than I want the comfort of my escape.

You are my safe place. Even when I can't feel it yet.
In Jesus' name,
Amen.

Journal Prompt:

What is your "go-to" when you're overwhelmed, stressed or emotionally exhausted? Be honest. Is it food, social media, busyness, sarcasm, shopping, alcohol, control.. something else?

In what ways has that habit brought temporary comfort but long-term distance between you and God? How has it affected your prayer life, your peace, or your sense of purpose?

When was the last time you asked God to meet you in that moment of temptation? What do you think would happen if you did?

SAFE WHEN YOU'RE SPIRITUALLY EXHAUSTED

"Come to Me, all who are weary and burdened, and I will give you rest." Matthew 11:28 (NASB)

When You're Running on Empty

You love Jesus, desperately, and You pray. and You worship. and yes.. of course You show up.

But you're tired.

No.. it's more than that... you're *soul-tired*.

And not just from a bad night's sleep or a full calendar. This is the kind of tired that sits in your bones. That makes your eyes heavy in worship. That whispers, *I can't do this anymore,* even while you're still doing it.

This kind of exhaustion doesn't always come from doing "bad" things. Sometimes it comes from doing all the *right* things , on autopilot, with no rest in between. Sometimes you don't even realize you've drifted into burnout until you're there, sitting in your Sunday best with nothing left in your tank.

You look around at people who seem to be thriving in their faith, and all you can do is wonder why your spirit feels so dry.

My Sweet Friend.... You've Been Carrying Too Much

You've been strong for too long.

You've been the one people count on, the one who answers the call, leads the prayer, serves the team, carries the burden, encourages others... while inside, you're breaking down.

You've prayed for people with fire while your own prayers feel like ashes.

You've shown up for every service, every volunteer request, every group chat, been present for every emergency, and now you wonder why being around God's people makes you feel more drained than filled.

Let me say this with all the gentleness in the world, i will even hold your hand:

You are not a bad Christian for needing a break.

You are not less holy because your soul is crying out for rest.

You are human.

And Jesus has never once called you to be a machine. But He has called you to *abide in Him*.

Let's talk about the lie of perpetual motion.

Church culture can sometimes unintentionally glorify *over-functioning*. We equate faithfulness with busyness. We assume a full schedule means a full heart. But running around in service of God doesn't mean you're walking with Him.

Sometimes we serve out of overflow.

Other times we serve out of obligation.

And if we're not careful, the altar we built for God becomes an idol of performance. (that one hurts a little bit...)

You were never meant to hustle your way into God's approval.

You already have it.

Before you served. Before you sang. Before you "showed up."

Jesus said, *Come to Me, all who are weary and burdened, and I will give you rest.*

He didn't say "Come when you've earned it."

He just said "Come."

So what do you do when the fire feels dim?

Spiritual exhaustion is sneaky. It doesn't always look like crisis. It often looks like subtle disconnection. Like numbness in your spirit. Like praising God with your mouth while your heart is frozen.

It looks like:

- Dreading church but going anyway.
- Reading Scripture but not remembering a word.

- Playing worship music but feeling nothing.
- Nodding through sermons with a heart full of questions.

You're not fake.

You're just tired.

And maybe what your soul needs right now isn't more striving.

Maybe what your soul needs is to **collapse into grace**.

Here you go... some manna for today.

Remember the Israelites in the wilderness? God gave them **manna**, daily bread just enough for each day.

Not a month's supply.

Not an advanced menu.

Just enough.

Maybe you're in a wilderness season. Maybe everything feels unfamiliar and exhausting. But the good news is: you have a God who gives **daily grace**, not performance-based reward. He's not asking you to be strong for a year , just *to come to Him today*.

Just today.

Just start with today..

What If You Told the Truth?

What if you stopped trying to fake your way through faith and just... told the truth?

"I'm spiritually tired."

"I'm not hearing God like I used to."

"I'm scared I've drifted."

"I don't feel like praying. I don't feel much of anything."

What if that honesty didn't disqualify you, what if it was the very thing that unlocked your healing?

The truth is <u>SAFE</u> in God's presence.

Your confession isn't a threat to Him. It's a doorway to intimacy. The truth always is.

Did you know? Rest Is Worship Too

Sometimes the most spiritual thing you can do is **take a nap.**

Or take a break.

Or log off.

Or go outside and breathe.

Or sit in silence without a single verse or lyric and just *be* with God.

You don't have to perform to belong.

You don't have to earn His rest.

You are loved in your stillness.

Let the stillness become a sanctuary.

You Are Still Safe Here

Jesus never turned away the weary.

He healed the woman with the issue of blood, it was by her sheer will that her faith made her whole.

He sat with the grieving sisters.

He invited the burdened to His table.

And He's still doing it now.

He is not asking you to fake joy or manufacture zeal.

He is saying, "Come to Me. I will give you rest."

You are still cherished.

You are still safe.

Even here.

Especially here.

Exactly right here.

Prayer: For the One Who's Spiritually Exhausted
Jesus, I'm worn out.

Not just physically, but deep down where nobody sees. My spirit feels tired. My heart feels heavy. My mind won't stop racing. And my faith, the thing that used to anchor me, feels distant and dull.

I want to feel You again. I want to *want* You again. I want to rest without guilt and collapse into Your arms without having to prove my worth.

I lay down the pressure. I lay down the performance. I lay down the version of me that thinks I have to be strong all the time.

Come find me here, God.

In the middle of this burnout. In the silence. In the sighs. In the questions I'm too tired to ask.

Remind me I'm safe in Your presence, even when I have nothing to give. Let my rest be worship.

Let my stillness be sacred.

Let this season be where You rebuild me , not by force, but by love.

You're still here. I believe that. Even tired, I believe that.

And that is enough for today. hold me Jesus, hide me in Your shadow.

In Jesus' name,
Amen.

Journal Prompt:

When was the last time you felt truly connected to God? What was different about that season?

What has been drainin your spiritual energy lately, and what (or who) have you been turning to?

Write a prayer asking God to meet you in your exhaustion without shame, and to gently restore your faith.

Safe in the Stretch (From Faith to Faith)

"For in it the righteousness of God is revealed from faith to faith; as it is written: 'But the righteous one will live by faith.'" Romans 1:17 (NASB)

Stretching Faith Hurts... But It Heals

Let's be real: stretch season is *not* the same thing as "glow up" season.

Stretching doesn't feel like growth.

It feels like growing pains.

It feels like pressure, resistance, cracking knees, tired hands, and holding poses you never wanted to try.

Spiritually, it's the season where you're not backsliding... but you're also not *soaring*.

You're suspended somewhere in between.

God feels distant.

The prayers feel flat.

The miracles aren't lining up with your expectations.

But there's something deeper happening in the tension ,because God doesn't stretch things He's not planning to use.

You Might Not Feel Stronger... But You Are

Stretching seasons sneak up on you.

It might look like:

- A relationship you thought would last falling apart.

- A job that once fulfilled you suddenly becoming draining.

- An opportunity closing that seemed perfect.
- Praying for healing… and still waking up with pain.
- Saying yes to God — and then watching everything fall apart.

You question everything.

"Did I really hear God?"

"Am I failing?"

"Did I do something wrong?"

"Why does it feel like I'm going backward?"

But what if what you're calling a setback is actually a **stretch**?

Because from the outside, the stretch looks like strain.

But in the spirit, it's **strength training.**

You're being pulled beyond your comfort zone to grow into your **calling zone.**

From Faith to Faith … Not From Faith to Comfort

Let's break this verse down:

"From faith… to faith."

It doesn't say:

- "From faith to feelings."
- "From faith to clarity."
- "From faith to everything going your way."

Nope.

Just **faith to faith.**

Because spiritual growth isn't about seeing more , it's about trusting deeper.

It's about standing on a Word even when the world shakes.

It's about praising before the breakthrough.

It's about obeying when it makes *no earthly sense.*

Stretching takes you from head knowledge to **heart surrender.**

When the Faith You Had Isn't Enough for Where You're Going

Here's the kicker: the faith that got you *here* might not be strong enough to carry you *there.*

And that's okay.

This is where God upgrades your faith, not by magic, but through *pressure.*

You outgrow surface prayers.

You learn to listen longer.

You start to trust when God says "no", or worse, when He says nothing at all.

You stop needing to control it.

You stop needing to explain it.

You start leaning into a Savior who doesn't owe you answers, but gives you *presence.*

And sometimes, that presence shows up in fire.

Faith That Stretches Will Set You Ablaze

Ask Shadrach, Meshach, and Abednego what the stretch looked like.

It looked like a *furnace.* Seven times hotter than before.

But guess what? God didn't rescue them before the fire.

He *joined them inside of it.*

Stretching seasons may not deliver you from the heat, but they will reveal the One who walks with you in it.

When you walk out, you won't even smell like smoke.

Because stretched faith is **refined faith**.

It Feels Risky... Because It Is

Stretching will cost you something.

It might cost you:

- Your reputation.
- Your five-year plan.
- Your comfort zone.
- The approval of people who liked the "old you" better.
- The illusion of control.

But what you gain?

- Deeper dependence on God.
- Clearer spiritual vision.
- Peace that makes no sense.
- Radical obedience.
- An unshakable, *mature* faith.

That kind of faith can't be faked.

It can't be mimicked.

And it can't be built without the **stretch**.

What If You're Not Being Punished...

What if (stay with me here...) You're Being Prepared?

Stop calling it punishment when God is prepping you for something greater.

You're not in trouble.

You're in **training**.

He's building the muscles of trust, the tendons of patience, and the backbone of bold obedience.

Faith that stretches can carry other people.

It can withstand storms.

It can walk into dark places and still shine.

He's strengthening you for the weight of what's coming.

So don't despise the stretch.

Stay in it. Breathe through it. Don't run.

Let Him stretch your faith ... and *grow your future.*

Prayer for the One Who's Being Stretched
Father,
I'm uncomfortable. This season hurts. I feel like I'm holding things together with duct tape and one last hallelujah.
It's hard to feel safe when nothing is secure. But I trust that You are not punishing me ,You are *preparing* me.
You're pulling me from shallow belief into soul-deep trust.
You're inviting me into a new level of faith that doesn't need to see, to believe.
God, I surrender to the stretch.
Stretch my patience. Stretch my prayers. Stretch my vision. Stretch my obedience. Stretch my praise ... even when I don't see progress.
Help me remember I'm safe, even here.
Because I'm not alone. And You don't stretch what You won't strengthen. You are faithful in the fire. You are good in the gap.
And You are enough when everything else is uncertain.
Take me from faith to faith.
Let me come out of this season stronger, and *more surrendered*.
In Jesus' name,
Amen.

Journal Prompts:

What does "from faith to faith" mean to you personally? What does the next step of faith look like?

Are you more afraid of failing or more afraid of letting go of control? Why? Are you willing to trust God even when you can't trace Him? What stops you?

Write a letter to your "future self" a year from now, from the faith you hope to be walking in. Be bold. Be honest. Be expectant.

SAFE IN THE VICTORY YOU DIDN'T EXPECT

"But thanks be to God, who always leads us in triumph in Christ, and manifests through us the sweet aroma of the knowledge of Him in every place." 2 Corinthians 2:14 (NASB)

Victory Looks Different Now

You thought victory would look like a mountaintop. But it looked more like crawling out of bed when you didn't want to.

It looked like not replying to that text.

It looked like finally crying after months of being numb.

It looked like *staying* when everything in you wanted to run.

It didn't feel like fireworks.

It felt like oxygen after nearly drowning.

You thought the win would come with confetti. Instead, it came with quiet strength.

And that? That's still victory. A bigger one than you think..

Newsflash sweet friend...Victory Isn't Always Loud

We tend to think of victory as loud like headlines on the front page...

The disease is gone. The marriage is saved. The bill is paid. The prodigal comes home. And when that happens ? Yes, let's shout!

But what about the silent victories?

Choosing to forgive someone who never apologized.

Walking away from what you *thought* you needed.

Lifting your hands in worship even though your heart is still healing.

Speaking truth when it shakes your voice.

Choosing faith on a day you didn't feel it.

<u>Those count too.</u>

God sees victories we don't post about.

Heaven celebrates strength we didn't know we had.

And your small win? It echoes in eternity.

You Didn't Feel It ... But It Counted

Let's be real: sometimes victory doesn't feel victorious at all.

Sometimes you're still sad, still scarred, still sore ; but you've moved forward anyway.

That prayer you whispered even though you felt hollow? **Victory.**

That temptation you said "not today" to? **Victory.**

That trauma you finally named? **Victory.**

That text you deleted instead of sending? **Victory.**

That lie you refused to agree with in your mind? **Victory.**

You didn't need trumpets. You needed *truth*.

And the truth is: you're winning more battles than you think.

Winning Without the Applause

Maybe no one clapped when you walked away from the addiction.

Maybe your family didn't notice when you broke that generational curse.

Maybe your friends didn't know you finally stood up to the lie that's haunted you for years.

But God saw it.

The kingdom of darkness saw it.

Hell trembled when you whispered *Jesus* instead of spiraling.

Heaven rejoiced when you chose peace instead of panic.

The angels leaned in when you said, "Even if it doesn't change, I'll still trust You." You don't need a crowd to validate your win.

You only need the One who conquered death to call you victorious and guess what?? He already has.

Safe in the Aftermath

Sometimes the scariest part isn't the battle , it's *after* the win.

What do I do now?

Will it come back?

Was that just adrenaline?

Am I strong enough to keep this up?

Victory is holy ground, but it's also vulnerable.

You finally *did the thing*... and now your knees feel weak.

That's okay.

You don't have to be perfect in the aftermath.

You don't have to maintain some polished image of "the healed version of you."

You can rest here.

Let God be your safety *after* the win too.

Let Him remind you that your identity is not in how strong you stay , it's in who you belong to.

Testimony in Progress

You are living proof that survival can be sacred.

That grief doesn't cancel glory.

That healing can be holy even when it's messy.

You are a walking testimony ;not because you did everything right, but because God stayed faithful when you didn't.

You are here. That's a miracle.

Don't minimize the wins that no one sees.

Don't wait for a "big moment" to say you've overcome.

You already have.

Prayer: For the One Who's Quietly Winning
Jesus,
Thank You that victory doesn't always have to be loud. Thank You that I don't have to wave a flag or make a post for it to be real. Some of my wins came through tears. Some through gritted teeth. Some through shaking hands and silent prayers. But they were still *wins*.
Thank You for walking with me in every battle I thought would break me. Thank You for calling me victorious even when I still feel fragile.
Remind me that You see every inch of progress, even when no one else does. Remind me that Your Spirit is the reason I could keep going.
Today, I want to stop and praise You for the victories I almost missed:
The anxiety that didn't win today.
The temptation that lost.
The curse that broke.
The fear that didn't get the last word.
The lie I finally laid down.
God, teach me to celebrate without shame.
Teach me to rest without fear.
And when the next battle comes, remind me , I've already overcome through You.
In Jesus' name,
Amen.

Journal Prompts

What does victory look like for you right now? (it may not be fireworks and big wins, maybe it's just getting out of bed today)

Has God brought you through something recently that you haven't taken the time to celebrate? How can you mark that moment?

What battles did you think would destroy you, but God turned into testimonies?

Safe in Salvation

"The Lord is not slow about His promise, as some count slowness, but is patient toward you, not willing for any to perish, but for all to come to repentance." 2 Peter 3:9 (NASB)

"The Lord will fight for you, while you keep silent." Exodus 14:14 (NASB)

When Letting Go Leads to Coming Home

There's this moment , this holy, gut-wrenching, knee-buckling moment , when you realize:

You're not just tired.

You're *lost*.

Not in the way the world defines it.

You've known about God. Maybe even served Him, loved Him, worshipped Him in the ways you were taught.

But you've been carrying your own salvation like a weight. Trying to be enough. Do enough. Know enough.

And still... the void won't close.

Until now.

Because surrender isn't the end.

It's the beginning.

And it leads straight into **salvation** , the safest place you will ever know.

When You've Reached the End of Yourself

Maybe Day 1 felt easy.

Maybe you loved journaling through the early chapters of healing, hiding, rebuilding, and surviving.

But by now?

You've peeled back so many layers that your soul feels like it's standing naked before God.

Good.

Because *this* is the part where He stops being a concept, and starts being your **Savior**.

Maybe you've said the words before. Maybe you've prayed a salvation prayer at youth camp, or in the back of a church pew, or whispered into a tear-stained pillow.

But maybe this time... it's different.

Maybe this time, you're not just repeating a prayer.

You're *giving Him your life. Thats no small thing.*

Surrender First. Then Salvation.

Let's talk about what no one says enough:

You can be around God and still not know Him.

You can serve Him and still not be saved.

You can fake freedom so well that even you believe it, until the storm hits.

And that's when everything breaks open.

You stop trying to prove yourself.

You stop performing.

You stop bargaining, justifying, controlling.

And you whisper those world-shaking, eternity-breaking words:

"Jesus, I need You. I can't do this without You. Save me."

That's salvation.

It doesn't have to come in a sanctuary.

It can come in the wreckage.

It can come in the silence after a suicide attempt.

It can come after the abortion.

After the overdose.

After the affair.

After the breakdown.

After you've run from every altar and every truth.

And still , Jesus calls you **home. Why?**

Because He loves you. simple and yet so hard to grasp.

Because His love is limitless, reckless, uncontrolled, untamed, wild,and absolute for you.

What You're Really Being Saved From

You're not being saved from just a hard life.

You're not being saved from sadness, or bills, or heartbreak.

You're being saved from the **eternal separation** between you and the God who made you.

You're being rescued from the death sentence of sin, not because you're perfect, but because **Jesus is and He took your place.**

> "But God demonstrates His own love toward us, in that while we were still sinners, Christ died for us." Romans 5:8 (NASB)

You're being saved from being forever apart from Love.

From your own self judgment and the curse of sin.

From the lies of the enemy who tried to convince you you'd never be worthy.

You're not just "getting a new start."

You're receiving a new **identity**.

And What You're Being Saved Into

Salvation isn't just a rescue ... it's a rebirth.

You get a *new name*.

A *new heart*.

A *new Spirit* living inside of you.

A *new future* sealed with a promise.

You become the righteousness of God in Christ Jesus.

You are adopted into His family.

You are filled with the power of the Holy Spirit.

That is not religion. That is resurrection.

This is where faith isn't just something you believe; it's something that *revives* you.

Where life begins, where hope resides, where mercies are renewed every morning, and where grace covers you.

What If You Already Know Him, But Need to Come Home?

This is for the one who's been walking with God but lost the intimacy.

The one who has drifted so far you barely recognize your own voice in prayer.

The one who has done all the "right" things and still feels cold.

Come home.

God doesn't shame the prodigal.

He runs to you.

He prepares a feast.

He covers your mess in robes of righteousness.

He silences the lies that say, *"You blew it."*

He says, *"Welcome back, son or daughter, I missed you."*

He has seen you, wept for you, called for you, and yearned for this moment.

This Is Your Invitation

This is your Day 30.

Not the end , the beginning.

Let everything before this moment fall silent.

Let Heaven listen.

If you want to receive Jesus, really receive Him,

If you're tired of trying to be enough

If you're done running

If you're ready to be *safe* for real...

Then pray this with me.

Prayer of Surrender and Salvation
Jesus,
I surrender.
Not part of me, all of me.
I believe You are the Son of God.
I believe You died on the cross for my sin.
I believe You rose from the dead. And I believe that You ,and You alone, can save me.
So I'm asking You right now:
Save me. Rescue me. Redeem me. Make me new.
I give You my heart. I give You my past.
I give You the future I was terrified to trust You with.
Come live in me.
Be my Lord.
Be my Savior.
Be my safety.
And when I wander, call me back.
When I doubt, remind me I'm Yours.
When I break, rebuild me with Your love.
I'm not perfect.
But I'm Yours.
In Jesus' name,
Amen.

Journal Prompts:

Have you truly received salvation for yourself, or just lived near it?

What fears or lies have kept you from fully giving your life to jesus, or coming back home?

Write your salvation story, whether it happened today or years ago, then write a prayer of gratitude for your eternal safety in Him.

FINAL WORD: YOU ARE FOREVER SAFE

If you just prayed that , for the first time or for the thousandth,

Heaven is rejoicing. Hell lost a soul today.

And you gained eternity.

You are not what you've done. You are not what was done to you.

You are not your shame. You are not your past.

You are now a daughter. A son.

A child of the Most High.

Sealed, secured, and *safe*.

Welcome Home

Jesus,

Look at this precious soul.

The one holding this book like it holds pieces of their own heart.

The one who didn't quit halfway through.

The one who showed up, even when they were tired, scared, numb, or angry.

The one who whispered yes to healing, even when it hurt.

God, You see them.

Every tear.

Every journal entry.

Every night they laid in bed and wondered if any of this was working.

Every whispered prayer they didn't think was holy enough.

Every time they asked, "Where are You?" and kept seeking anyway.

Father, I thank You that You've never once let them walk alone.

Not through the sorrow.

Not through the stretch.

Not through the silence.

And definitely not through the surrender.

You held them through every day of this devotional and You're not done yet.

Now I ask You, in the name of Jesus Christ, the resurrected King, the God who doesn't just patch wounds but **resurrects hearts**:

Finish the work You started.

Heal what's still bleeding.

Restore what was stolen.

Light a fire that never goes out.

And wrap them in the kind of safety that this world can't give and hell can't steal.

May they know, deep in their bones, that **salvation is their security**.

That **Your Word is their weapon**.

That **Your presence is their place of safety**.

And that **no weapon formed against them will ever prosper** because **they belong to You**.

Lord, for the person who still doubts their worth…

Show them they're loved.

Show them they're chosen.

Show them that they are dangerous to the kingdom of darkness ,because they are safe in the arms of Light.

Break every lie.

Shatter every chain.

Rebuild every broken place into a holy altar.

Let this not be the end of their healing, but the beginning of a revival.

Fill them with Your Spirit.

Lead them with Your peace.

Protect them with Your angels.

Speak to them with Your Word.

And empower them with Your purpose.

This is not just a devotional. This is a turning point.

This is not just a workbook. This is a **weapon**.

This is not just a book. This is a **battle cry.**

They are not the same person who started this.

They are grounded.

They are covered.

They are surrendered.

They are saved.

They are **safe.**

And the gates of hell will not prevail.

In the powerful, unshakable, victorious name of Jesus

Amen.

Forever Grateful

To my Scrunchy Saints, my framily, my heartbeat in this wild digital world.

Brittany, Jeanna, Christen, Char, Paula, Vicki, Wynona, Jess, Trina, Mckenzie, Britt, Lauren, Courtnie, Dachon, Taylor, jillian and so so many more..

I can't begin to express what you've meant to me. You've carried me in prayer when I couldn't stand. You've spoken life when my voice trembled. You've shown me the tangible love of Jesus through every comment, message, and late-night prayer chain. You've turned ordinary moments into sacred ground and made this space feel like home.

You are living proof that the Holy Spirit moves through Wi-Fi and phone screens, that community can be built on compassion and crowned with grace. You are the hands and feet of Jesus in messy buns and coffee cups, in laughter that heals and tears that intercede.

Every one of you reflects the heart of God. The way you show up for each other, the way you love without condition, the way you pray like you expect Heaven to move, it leaves me undone.

May this community continue to be a sanctuary for the weary and a celebration for the faithful. May everyone who crosses paths with the Scrunchy Saints encounter the kind of love that ruins them for anything less than Jesus.

I am forever grateful for you. For your hearts. For your faith. For the fire you carry.

And I pray that none of us, none who join us, none who scroll by, none who whisper amen, ever stay the same.

With all my love and deepest gratitude,

Cyd

About the Author

Hi, it feels wierd to write about myself.. and now that sounds silly but i am just going for it here.

My name is Cynthia Oliver , I am a writer, a nurse, and a Jesus lover, momma to 2, Honey to 1 (almost 2), and a small town girl from north Texas.

I don't write from the mountaintop; I write from the middle, the messy, sacred middle where faith gets tested, laughter feels like warfare, and prayer sounds a lot like survival. I try to write words that are soaked in honesty, humor, and holy rebellion against fear itself.

I met Jesus truly, walking through one of the wildest, darkest and traumatic times in my life. I was blessed with a wild, beautiful "found family" of believers who show up for each other with coffee, scripture, and laughter in equal measure. Together, they've created a space for me to reside, to rest, and to create, a holy ground, proving that Jesus can meet us anywhere even in elementary school cafeterias.

My mission is simple: to remind the weary that God still moves, the broken that beauty still grows, and the fighters that victory is already theirs.

I don't want to build platforms for selfish gain, I want to build altars. Places where people can encounter the realness of God and remember they're not alone. A place where belonging is real, and His love proves your purpose always.

www.ingramcontent.com/pod-product-compliance
Lightning Source LLC
Chambersburg PA
CBHW071109160426
43196CB00013B/2517